Teacher's Guide

SPELL IT OUT

READING AND SPELLING PRACTICE

Phillip K. Trocki

BLUE LEVEL	RED LEVEL
ORANGE LEVEL	PURPLE LEVEL

GLOBE BOOK COMPANY
A DIVISION OF SIMON & SCHUSTER
New York/Cleveland/Toronto/Sydney/Tokyo/Singapore

ISBN 1-55675-353-5

Published simultaneously in Canada by Globe/Modern Curriculum Press.

Printed in the United States of America

10 9 8 7 6 5 4 3 2 1

Contents

SPELL IT OUT—BOOK 1

SPELL IT OUT—BOOK 2

SPELL IT OUT—BOOK 3

SPELL IT OUT—BOOK 4

Introduction

Our primary goal as teachers of English is to help develop literate human beings. Literacy is defined simply as the ability to read and write. Certainly we are all aware that this is not a simple task. *Spell It Out* has been designed to develop skills in reading and in spelling because spelling is such an essential part of the written word. Spelling, in fact, is often the mark of a literate person.

The link between spelling and reading is clear. In part, spelling is a function of experience. The more experience the student has with the written word, the easier it will be for the student to learn the spelling of a word. Conversely, if the student has learned to spell a word and has gained practice in using the word in context, there will be benefits to the student in improved reading comprehension. *Spell It Out* reinforces the link between reading and spelling.

The short, high-interest reading selections have been carefully chosen to motivate the student. These reading selections, written at a low reading level, are particularly designed to motivate the student who is reading below grade level. It is felt that the interest engendered by the reading selections will carry over to the spelling lessons. These spelling lessons have been designed to provide both structure and diversity, in order to maintain interest and achieve success.

The *Spell It Out* series has been especially designed to aid students who have had negative experiences in spelling. The series approaches spelling with the premise that the poor reader is very often a poor speller. This premise is based on the fact that spelling a word is much more difficult than reading a word, and requires a certain expertise not always found in other disciplines where creativity and original thinking are stressed.

This program deals with the learning of spelling skills on a step-by-step basis, and capitalizes on the phonetic regularities that exist within our language. Each lesson presents a rule and a list of words that apply to that rule, thus encouraging the student to make linguistic generalizations that will apply over and over again. With this technique, the student is given the opportunity to draw conclusions about the similarities and differences within a word and is asked to make associations based on predictable spelling patterns.

The ability to spell is naturally based on the ability to learn. Fortunately, the approach to learning is not the same for every student, and must be dealt with on an individual basis. *Spell It Out* does this in asking students to copy, rewrite, proofread, define, and write from memory. Many different channels of learning are presented for the many different ways students learn.

Structure of Lessons

Reading. Each reading selection is followed by reading comprehension questions designed to develop the following skills:

Reading for Details   Improving Vocabulary
Identifying Sequence   Finding the Main Idea
   of Events   Making Inferences

The "What's Your Opinion?" section that follows the reading skill exercises provides an opportunity for the student to develop skills in constructing sentences and expressing complete thoughts. In a sense, this exercise allows the student to "talk back" to the book.

Spelling. Each spelling section introduces 15 words that are exemplary of a spelling pattern or rule. Some of the words used to demonstrate the rule are taken from the reading selection. This provides an opportunity for the teacher to link the spelling words and the reading selection. It also allows the students to see some of the words that illustrate the rule or pattern used in the context of the story.

The spelling exercises are predicated on the belief that students require both structure and drill to master spelling skills. The spelling rules or patterns provide the structure. They allow the student to look for the particular pattern that may cause the word to be hard to spell. At least one of the "Skill Drills" emphasizes the usual trouble spots in spelling the "Study List" words. The "Skill Drills" that follow the explanation of the spelling pattern provide the practice the student needs to develop spelling mastery.

At the end of each lesson there is a review exercise entitled "How Well Can You Spell?" This exercise may be used as a test of the students' mastery of the spelling words, since the "Study List" does not appear on this page or on the facing page.

The time for students to develop spelling skills is while they are developing the basics of intellectual growth. Certainly spelling is an indication of the level of a person's literacy. Once well learned, correct spelling will remain an invaluable part of the student's intellect—for life.

Scope and Sequence of Lessons

Organization of Skills

The *Spell It Out* series has been specifically designed for consistent instruction throughout the three volumes. Each of the skills listed are in all three books and appear at the same place in each book. Therefore, the page numbers listed below are consistent for all three volumes. Naturally, each volume advances in reading level and degree of difficulty. The following list of skills and page numbers is the same for *Spell It Out-Books 1, 2, and 3.*

MAIN IDEA

2, 10, 18, 26, 34, 42, 50, 58, 66, 74, 82, 90, 98, 106, 114, 122, 130, 138, 146, 154

SEQUENCE OF EVENTS

2, 10, 18, 26, 34, 42, 50, 58, 66, 74, 82, 90, 98, 106, 114, 122, 130, 138, 146, 154

DRAWING CONCLUSIONS

3, 11, 19, 27, 35, 43, 51, 59, 67, 75, 83, 91, 99, 107, 115, 123, 131, 139, 147, 155

FOLLOWING DIRECTIONS

7, 15, 23, 31, 39, 47, 55, 63, 71, 79, 87, 95, 103, 111, 119, 127, 135, 143, 151, 159

APPLICATION OF IDEAS

3, 11, 19, 27, 35, 43, 51, 59, 67, 75, 83, 91, 99, 107, 115, 123, 131, 139, 147, 155

UNDERSTANDING RELATIONSHIPS AND CLASSIFYING IDEAS

5-6, 13-14, 21-22, 29-30, 37-38, 45-46, 53-54, 61-62, 69-70, 77, 93, 109-110, 125-126, 133-134, 141, 149, 157

DETAIL

2, 10, 18, 26, 34, 42, 50, 58, 66, 74, 82, 90, 98, 106, 114, 122, 130, 138, 146, 154

LOGIC AND REASONING SKILLS

3, 11, 19, 27, 35, 43, 51, 59, 67, 75, 83, 91, 99, 101, 107, 115, 117, 123, 131, 139, 147, 155

PHONETIC ANALYSIS

46-47, 77-78, 79, 86-87

DRAWING INFERENCES

2, 10, 18, 26, 34, 42, 50, 58, 66, 74, 82, 90, 98, 106, 114, 122, 130, 138, 146, 154

STRUCTURAL ANALYSIS

5-6, 13-14, 21-22, 29-30, 38-39, 45-46, 53-54, 61-62, 69-70, 93-94, 101-102, 109-110, 117-118, 126, 133, 141-142, 150-151, 158-159

WRITING SKILLS

3, 11, 19, 27, 35, 43, 51, 59, 67, 75, 83, 91, 99, 107, 115, 123, 131, 139, 147, 155

SPELLING RULES

4, 12, 20, 28, 36, 44, 52, 60, 68, 76, 84, 92, 100, 108, 116, 124, 132, 140, 148, 156

Format of Guide and Answer Key

The format of the *Guide and Answer Key* is outlined below:
— Objective of the lesson combined with an explanation of the spelling rule or pattern
— Detailed list of answers
— One or more additional activities relevant to the lesson
— List of supplementary words pertaining to the rule for added reinforcement
— Optional testing list for every five lessons

If there is more than one answer to a question in the "Skill Drills," the answers have been arranged in alphabetical order for your convenience. NOTE: When students write their answers, some might not always list them alphabetically. If they have listed all the appropriate words they should not be penalized.

Spell It Out—Book 1
Sample Lesson Plan

Captain Fantastic
Pages 1–8

Objectives

Improving reading skills by finding the main idea, remembering details, and making inferences through experience and exercises.

Learning the double-consonant pattern in words through the memorization and writing of 15 words.

Motivation

For this lesson, you might want to select a short piece of classical music and an Elton John recording. Play both of them for the class. Then question the students to evoke comparisons between the two. Since the reading selection mentions classical music as essential to Elton John's development as a musician, it is only fitting that students listen to and compare both kinds of music.

Procedure

1. Have the students look at the picture on page 1. Ask: "Does anyone know who the person in the picture is? What does the picture tell you about him? Why do you think the selection is titled 'Captain Fantastic'?"

2. Have students read the story silently. Instruct them to turn the page and complete the "Reviewing Your Reading" and "Figuring the Facts" exercises.

3. Choose students to go back and read the story aloud. Then ask individual students to read and answer the questions orally. This will provide a participating activity and an answer check for all students.

4. Direct the students to answer the "What's Your Opinion?" exercise. This exercise can be used as a discussion activity or as a writing activity. If you choose to use it as a writing activity, have the students write one or two complete sentences on the lines provides. Follow up by having some students read their responses aloud and discuss the differences in their answers. Since these answers will vary, they will not appear in the answer key that follows.

5. Next, have the students turn to page 4. Explain that the words in dark type appear in the reading selection and they demonstrate a pattern that often appears in words—double consonants.

Your demonstration should include a review of consonants and vowels. Have the students underline the double consonants in each of the examples. Then point out the "Study List" that appears on the left of the page. It would be wise to review the meanings of all the "Study List" words with the class and instruct students to refer to the "Mini-Dictionary" (page 162 in the student book) to find definitions they are unsure of.

6. Direct the students to begin the series of "Skill Drills." The answers to the "Skill Drills" have been arranged in alphabetical order, where applicable, for your convenience. In "Skill Drill 4," page 6, for example, the students are required to list all the Study List words with a double *l*. The answer key lists the four words as: 1. college 2. excellent 3. million 4. syllable.

Since all of the "Skill Drills" require words from the "Study List" as answers, it is not necessary to assign the drills in order. You may wish to save more challenging drills and the "Word Game" to motivate follow-up lessons.

7. After the four "Skill Drills" and the "Word Game" have been completed and checked, direct the students to take the review on page 8, entitled "How Well Can You Spell?" You might want to have the students check their own work while you read the correct answers. This can be reinforcing because the students will have the opportunity to correct their own errors and thus strengthen their own knowledge of the words.

Follow Up

1. Have the students do research in recent periodicals on Elton John or other rock stars and prepare a short written or oral report.

2. Have students clip out a section of a newspaper or magazine. They should circle words with double consonants and make a list of the words they have found.

3. The traditional spelling bee and other "Word Games" such as those in *Spell It Out* are good reinforcements for a spelling lesson. Students can be encouraged to create their own puzzles and then share them with other class members. This kind of exercise will increase their vocabulary, as well as their spelling skill.

4. Every few lessons should be followed up by a test. Dictate each word clearly once. Then use each word in a sentence and repeat the word. Encourage students not to write until you have finished speaking.

Spell It Out—Book 1
Guide and Answer Key

1. Captain Fantastic

Pages 1–8

Objective

This lesson emphasizes improving reading skills by finding the main idea, remembering details, and making inferences. Students learn the double-consonant pattern in words through memorizing and writing 15 words.

REVIEWING YOUR READING

1. c   2. b   3. b   4. a   5. a   6. c   7. b   8. b

FIGURING THE FACTS

1. T   2. T   3. T   4. F   5. F   6. T   7. T   8. F   9. T
10. T

WHAT'S YOUR OPINION?

Answers will vary.

SKILL DRILL 1

1. glasses	2. excellent	3. unless	4. little	5. grammar
6. college	7. summer	8. soccer	9. syllable	10. pepper
11. address	12. beginning	13. million	14. disappear	15. classical

SKILL DRILL 2

1. pepper	2. summer	3. disappear	4. address	5. grammar
6. college and million	7. soccer	8. beginning	9. grammar	10. excellent
11. unless	12. syllable	13. classical	14. little	

SKILL DRILL 3

1. grammar	2. glasses	3. pepper	4. beginning	5. million
6. syllable	7. excellent	8. unless	9. little	10. address
11. college	12. summer	13. disappear	14. classical	15. soccer

SKILL DRILL 4

Order of answers may vary in 1–4, 5–6, 8–11, 12–13.

1. college	2. million	3. excellent	4. syllable	5. disappear
6. pepper	7. soccer	8. address	9. glasses	10. classical
11. unless	12. grammar	13. summer	14. little	15. beginning
16. address				

WORD GAME 1

The extra word is *EXTRA*.

HOW WELL CAN YOU SPELL?

A. 1. excellent   2. unless   3. college   4. summer   5. syllable
    6. beginning   7. disappear

B. 8. classical   9. glasses   10. million   11. address   12. pepper
    13. soccer   14. little   15. grammar

---

2. Lincoln's Ghost

Pages 9–16

Objective

This lesson deals with words that have consonants that are not normally heard when pronounced. We call these as *silent letters*. By emphasizing these as silent letters, the student will be more apt to focus on this often misspelled part of the word, and will be able to make generalizations about similar words. The teacher should point out that in the English language, these silent letters often appear in conjunction with another consonant, and usually only the additional consonant is sounded.

It may be of help to some students to pronounce these silent letters when memorizing the spelling of the words. Some researchers have found that when students deliberately mispronounce words while learning to spell them, they make a more meaningful mental impression of the accurate spelling of the word. For example, when studying the spelling of the word *listen*, a student is more apt to remember that there is a silent *t* if he or she makes a mental pronunciation of the word as *lis/TEN*. However, the teacher should make it clear to the student that this is not how the word should be pronounced in everyday conversation.

REVIEWING YOUR READING

1. d   2. a   3. c   4. c   5. b   6. b   7. c   8. d

FIGURING THE FACTS

1. F   2. T   3. F   4. T   5. T   6. T   7. F   8. F   9. F
10. T

WHAT'S YOUR OPINION?

Answers will vary.

SKILL DRILL 1

1. hour   2. column   3. ghost   4. might   5. lighten
6. hymn   7. solemn   8. whistle   9. autumn   10. frighten
11. through   12. often   13. condemn   14. castle   15. listen

SKILL DRILL 2

1. autumn   2. hour   3. column   4. ghost   5. lighten
6. hymn   7. through/ lighten   8. might   9. castle and listen   10. condemn
11. frighten   12. whistle   13. solemn   14. often

SKILL DRILL 3

1. often	**2.** solemn	**3.** whistle	**4.** condemn	**5.** listen
6. hour	**7.** column	**8.** ghost	**9.** might	**10.** listen
11. autumn	**12.** frighten	**13.** through	**14.** hymn	**15.** castle

SKILL DRILL 4

Order of answers may vary in 1–4, 5–8, 9–10, 11–14.

1. castle	**2.** often	**3.** listen	**4.** whistle	**5.** frighten
6. might	**7.** lighten	**8.** through	**9.** hour	**10.** whistle
11. autumn	**12.** hymn	**13.** column	**14.** solemn	**15.** condemn

WORD GAME 2

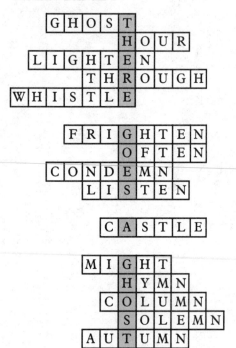

The hidden message is *THERE GOES A GHOST*.

HOW WELL CAN YOU SPELL?

A.

1. hour	**2.** column	**3.** ghost	**4.** might	**5.** lighten
6. hymn	**7.** condemn			

B.

8. whistle	**9.** autumn	**10.** frighten	**11.** through	**12.** often
13. solemn	**14.** listen	**15.** castle		

---

3. Sounds of Silence

Pages 17–24

Objective

As in Lesson 2, the emphasis here is on letters not normally heard when words are pronounced. In addition to letters introduced in the previous lesson, here we also have silent *b*, *w*, *d*, and *k*. Once again, the teacher should point out that these consonants usually appear in conjunction with another consonant, which is sounded.

REVIEWING YOUR READING
1. c   **2.** a   **3.** b   **4.** c   **5.** c   **6.** d   **7.** b   **8.** d

FIGURING THE FACTS
1. F   **2.** F   **3.** T   **4.** T   **5.** T   **6.** F   **7.** T   **8.** F   **9.** F
10. T

WHAT'S YOUR OPINION?
Answers will vary.

SKILL DRILL 1
1. knew	**2.** wrestle	**3.** comb	**4.** knife	**5.** wreck
6. knapsack	**7.** doubt	**8.** doorknob	**9.** thumb	**10.** knowledge
11. wrist	**12.** lamb	**13.** debt	**14.** wreath	**15.** wrong

SKILL DRILL 2
1. wreath	**2.** lamb	**3.** knowledge	**4.** doorknob	**5.** doubt
6. debt	**7.** wrist	**8.** thumb	**9.** wrong	**10.** knew
11. wreck	**12.** knife	**13.** comb	**14.** wrestle	**15.** knapsack

SKILL DRILL 3
Order of answers may vary in 1–4, 6–11, 12–15.
1. comb	**2.** lamb	**3.** debt	**4.** thumb	**5.** doubt
6. wreath	**7.** wrist	**8.** wreck	**9.** wrong	**10.** wrestle
11. knowledge	**12.** knew	**13.** knife	**14.** doorknob	**15.** knowledge
16. knapsack				

SKILL DRILL 4
1. debt	**2.** wrist	**3.** wrong	**4.** thumb	**5.** knew
6. doubt	**7.** doorknob	**8.** knowledge	**9.** lamb	**10.** wreath
11. knapsack	**12.** wrestle	**13.** comb	**14.** knife	**15.** wreck

WORD GAME 3

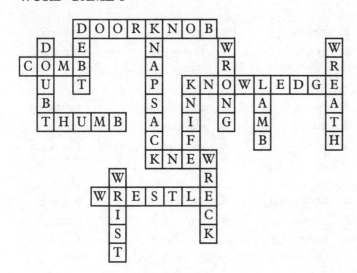

HOW WELL CAN YOU SPELL?

A. 1. knapsack 2. comb 3. wreck 4. doubt 5. thumb
  6. doorknob 7. wrestle

B. 8. knowledge 9. knife 10. lamb 11. wreaths 12. wrong
  13. debt 14. knew 15. wrist

---

4. Perfect Game

Pages 25–32

Objective

This lesson introduces the concept of *compound words*. It is the first step towards having the student break words down into smaller units. In most cases the student will be adequately prepared to spell the smaller components of a compound, but will be intimidated and deceived by the entire compound. The purpose of this lesson and the next is to dissect compounds into units that more easily facilitate spelling.

REVIEWING YOUR READING

1. a 2. c 3. c 4. c 5. b 6. b 7. a 8. b

FIGURING THE FACTS

1. T 2. F 3. F 4. F 5. T 6. T 7. T 8. T 9. T
10. F

WHAT'S YOUR OPINION?

Answers will vary.

SKILL DRILL 1

1. room mate 2. power house 3. some time 4. air plane 5. out side
6. with out 7. may be 8. every one 9. basket ball 10. pea nut
11. extra ordinary 12. base ball 13. knock out 14. home sick 15. an other

SKILL DRILL 2

1. basketball 2. knockout 3. airplane 4. peanut 5. homesick
6. powerhouse 7. without 8. maybe 9. baseball 10. extraordinary

SKILL DRILL 3

1. another 2. homesick 3. baseball 4. extraordinary 5. peanut
6. basketball 7. everyone 8. maybe 9. without 10. outside
11. airplane 12. sometime 13. powerhouse 14. roommate 15. knockout

SKILL DRILL 4

1. with/out 2. knock/out 3. basket/ball 4. every/one 5. out/side
6. pea/nut 7. extra/ordinary 8. may/be 9. home/sick 10. power/house
11. air/plane 12. room/mate 13. some/time 14. base/ball 15. an/other

WORD GAME 4

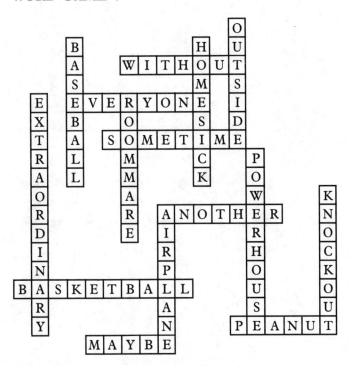

HOW WELL CAN YOU SPELL?

A. **1.** peanut **2.** sometime **3.** airplane **4.** homesick **5.** roommate

  6. disappear

B. **7.** another **8.** knockout **9.** basketball **10.** Maybe **11.** without

  12. outside **13.** Baseball **14.** powerhouse **15.** everyone

---

5. Good-time Charlie

Pages 33–40

Objective

As in the previous lesson, this chapter deals with compound words. The teacher should point out that compounds are words made up of two or more smaller words, which when joined together have a new meaning. The teacher may wish to use this lesson to point out that if students do not know the meaning of a word, they can often dissect the word and derive clues to the definition.

REVIEWING YOUR READING

 1. d **2.** b **3.** a **4.** a **5.** b **6.** b **7.** d **8.** c

FIRST THINGS FIRST

2, 1, 3, 5, 4

WHAT'S YOUR OPINION?

Answers will vary.

SKILL DRILL 1

1. fire house	**2.** any thing	**3.** rail road	**4.** motor cycle	**5.** some body
6. eye brow	**7.** him self	**8.** sail boat	**9.** snow ball	**10.** butter fly
11. pan cake	**12.** news paper	**13.** every body	**14.** battle ship	**15.** foot steps

SKILL DRILL 2

1. snowball	**2.** eyebrow	**3.** battleship	**4.** butterfly	**5.** railroad
6. pancake	**7.** footsteps	**8.** firehouse	**9.** newspaper	**10.** motorcycle

SKILL DRILL 3

1. sailboat	**2.** newspaper	**3.** butterfly	**4.** pancake	**5.** firehouse
6. eyebrow	**7.** everybody	**8.** battleship	**9.** himself	**10.** footsteps
11. anything	**12.** railroad	**13.** motorcycle	**14.** snowball	**15.** somebody

SKILL DRILL 4

anyone	anything	anywhere	anybody
everyone	everything	everywhere	everybody
someone	something	somewhere	somebody

WORD GAME 5

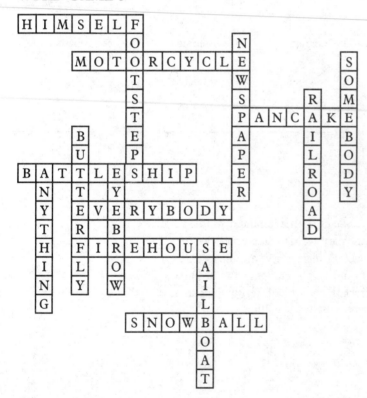

HOW WELL DO YOU SPELL?

A.
1. somebody	**2.** pancake	**3.** firehouse	**4.** eyebrow	**5.** battleship
6. footsteps	**7.** newspaper			

B.
8. anything	**9.** motorcycle	**10.** railroad	**11.** himself	**12.** everybody
13. butterfly	**14.** sailboat	**15.** snowball		

8

6. Walkman

Pages 41–48

Objective

In this chapter we introduce the concept of *prefixes*. The teacher should make certain that the student is aware that a prefix is a word part added to the beginning of a word or a base, and that each prefix has its own meaning. Knowledge of prefixes and their meanings is not only an aid to the student in spelling, but it is an integral part of vocabulary development. The teacher should encourage the student to seek out and commit to memory words that have the same prefixes. This provides a good opportunity for the student not only to strengthen spelling skills but to develop vocabulary as well.

REVIEWING YOUR READING

1. b   **2.** a   **3.** b   **4.** d   **5.** c   **6.** b   **7.** d   **8.** a

FIGURING THE FACTS

1. T   **2.** F   **3.** F   **4.** T   **5.** T   **6.** T   **7.** F   **8.** T   **9.** F
10. T

WHAT'S YOUR OPINION?

Answers will vary.

SKILL DRILL 1

1. com/bine   **2.** pre/fix   **3.** pre/pare   **4.** com/pare   **5.** pre/fer
6. un/able   **7.** en/close   **8.** un/tie   **9.** un/like   **10.** en/ter
11. en/force   **12.** com/plete   **13.** en/gage   **14.** com/bat   **15.** pre/vious

SKILL DRILL 2

Order of answers may vary in 1, 4, 12, 15; 2, 11, 13, 14; 3, 5, 6, 9; 7, 8, 10.

1. compare (combat, combine, compete)   **2.** previous (prepare, prefer, prefix)   **3.** engage (enter, enforce, enclose)   **5.** enter (enforce, enclose, engage)   **6.** enforce (enclose, engage, enter)   **7.** unable (unlike, untie)   **8.** unlike (untie, unable)   **9.** enclose (engage, enter, enforce)   **10.** untie (unable, unlike)   **11.** prepare (prefer, prefix, previous)   **12.** combine (compete, compare, combat)   **13.** prefer (prefix, previous, prepare)   **14.** prefix (previous, prepare, prefer)   **15.** compete (compare, combat, combine)

SKILL DRILL 3

1. combine   **2.** prefix   **3.** prepare   **4.** compare   **5.** prefer
6. enter   **7.** enforce   **8.** untie   **9.** engage   **10.** unlike
11. enclose   **12.** combat   **13.** unable   **14.** previous   **15.** compete

SKILL DRILL 4

Order of answers may vary in 1–3, 4–5, 6–7, 10–11.

1. combine   **2.** compete   **3.** compare   **4.** unlike   **5.** unable
6. enforce   **7.** enclose   **8.** untie   **9.** enter   **10.** prefer
11. prefix   **12.** combat   **13.** engage   **14.** previous   **15.** prepare

WORD GAME 6

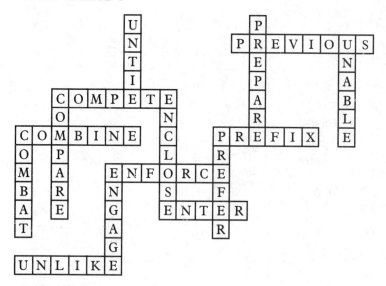

HOW WELL CAN YOU SPELL?

A. 1. combat   2. unlike   3. untie   4. combine   5. compare

   6. engage   7. prefer

B. 8. previous   9. unable   10. enter   11. enforce   12. enclose

   13. prefix   14. prepare   15. compete

---

7. The Alpine Slide
Pages 49–56

Objective
   Four more prefixes are introduced in this lesson, *dis, con, de,* and *pro.*
It would be most appropriate for the teacher to explain the different shades of
meaning that each of these prefixes carries. For example, the meaning of *dis*
in *discover* varies slightly from the meaning it infers in *disgrace.* The student
should be encouraged to become familiar with the dictionary definition of
each list word and to attempt to use each word in his or her writing.

REVIEWING YOUR READING
   1. c   2. b   3. c   4. a   5. d   6. d   7. c   8. b

FIGURING THE FACTS
   1. F   2. T   3. T   4. T   5. F   6. T   7. F   8. T   9. F
10. T

WHAT'S YOUR OPINION?
Answers will vary.

SKILL DRILL 1
   1. pro/pel   2. dis/cover   3. dis/grace   4. de/scend   5. de/tour

   6. con/fuse   7. pro/claim   8. con/trol   9. de/tect   10. pro/vide

   11. dis/turb   12. dis/agree   13. pro/duce   14. con/fer   15. con/ceal

SKILL DRILL 2

1. propel	2. discover	3. confuse	4. descend	5. detour
6. proclaim	7. provide	8. control	9. disgrace	10. detect
11. produce	12. disagree	13. disturb	14. confer	15. conceal

SKILL DRILL 3

1. produce	2. conceal	3. propel	4. discover	5. confuse
6. descend	7. detour	8. disagree	9. disgrace	10. confer
11. provide	12. disturb	13. control	14. detect	15. proclaim

SKILL DRILL 4

Order of answers may vary in 3–4, 5–8, 10–12.

1. proclaim	2. confer	3. produce	4. provide	5. detect
6. disagree	7. disgrace	8. discover	9. detour	10. conceal
11. control	12. confuse	13. propel	14. disturb	15. descend

WORD GAME 7

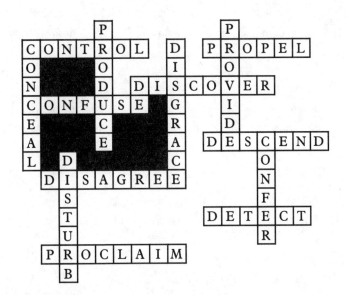

HOW WELL CAN YOU SPELL?

A.

1. proclaim	2. propel	3. disgrace	4. confer	5. confuse
6. conceal	7. detect			

B.

8. discover	9. control	10. descend	11. detour	12. disturb
13. provide	14. disagree	15. produce		

8. Baseball's Burglar

Pages 57–64

Objective

In this lesson, we first introduce the concept of *suffixes* and one of the most basic spelling rules: drop the final *e* when adding a suffix that begins with a vowel. The student should be knowledgeable of the fact that a suffix is a word part that is added to the end of a word or a base and that it is used to change the word from one part of speech to another. If at this point in the student's study of the English language there has not been an examination of the different parts of speech, it is necessary for the teacher to present one.

REVIEWING YOUR READING
1. b   **2.** c   **3.** c   **4.** d   **5.** c   **6.** b   **7.** c   **8.** a

FIGURING THE FACTS
1. T   **2.** T   **3.** F   **4.** T   **5.** F   **6.** T   **7.** F   **8.** T   **9.** T
10. T

WHAT'S YOUR OPINION?
Answers will vary.

Remind students that even though the suffix *ment* does not begin with a vowel, we drop the final *e* of *judge* to form *judgment*.

SKILL DRILL 1
1. shy/ness	**2.** advis/or	**3.** sweet/ness	**4.** treat/ment	**5.** govern/ment
6. radiat/or	**7.** judg/ment	**8.** weak/ness	**9.** creat/or	**10.** act/or
11. ill/ness	**12.** move/ment	**13.** supervis/or	**14.** appoint/ment	**15.** kind/ness

SKILL DRILL 2
1. shyness	**2.** appointment	**3.** weakness	**4.** treatment	**5.** sweetness
6. creator	**7.** judgment	**8.** advisor	**9.** illness	**10.** radiator
11. supervisor	**12.** government	**13.** actor	**14.** movement	**15.** kindness

SKILL DRILL 3
A.
1. treatment	**2.** supervisor	**3.** movement	**4.** actor	**5.** radiator
6. judgment	**7.** government	**8.** creator	**9.** appointment	**10.** advisor

B.
11. shyness	**12.** illness	**13.** kindness	**14.** sweetness	**15.** weakness

SKILL DRILL 4
Order of answers may vary in 2–5, 6–11, 12–13.
1. actor	**2.** advisor	**3.** government	**4.** movement	**5.** supervisor
6. treatment	**7.** radiator	**8.** appointment	**9.** creator	**10.** sweetness
11. weakness	**12.** judgment	**13.** kindness	**14.** illness	**15.** shyness

WORD GAME 8

```
      S W E E T N E S S
      T R E A T M E N T
  M O V E M E N T
      A D V I S O R
      I L L N E S S
S U P E R V I S O R
      K I N D N E S S
  J U D G M E N T

      R A D I A T O R
  W E A K N E S S
    A P P O I N T M E N T
    A C T O R
    S H Y N E S S
G O V E R N M E N T
    C R E A T O R
```

What will Rickey Henderson be doing after stealing a base? *STEALING ANOTHER*

HOW WELL CAN YOU SPELL?

A. 1. creator 2. supervisor 3. government 4. appointment 5. sweetness

   6. weakness 7. treatment

B. 8. movement 9. advisor 10. judgment 11. actor 12. illness

   13. radiator 14. shyness 15. kindness

---

9. An Old Twist

Pages 65–72

Objective

This lesson introduces the use of four more suffixes, *ion, er, able,* and *ly.* Once again the spelling rule, drop the final *e* when adding a suffix that begins with a vowel, is stressed. Also, the focus is on changing words from one part of speech to another. The teacher should use this lesson to review the identification of nouns, verbs, adjective, and adverbs.

REVIEWING YOUR READING

1. b 2. a 3. c 4. d 5. d 6. a 7. b 8. a

FIGURING THE FACTS

1. T 2. F 3. T 4. F 5. T 6. T 7. F 8. T 9. T
10. F

WHAT'S YOUR OPINION?

Answers will vary.

SKILL DRILL 1

1. depend/able
2. glad/ly
3. deep/ly
4. comfort/able
5. high/ly
6. prevent/ion
7. play/er
8. creat/ion
9. sure/ly
10. speak/er
11. teach/er
12. bak/er
13. avail/able
14. act/ion
15. work/er

SKILL DRILL 2

1. deeply
2. comfortable
3. dependable
4. surely
5. baker
6. worker
7. available
8. player
9. action
10. teacher
11. speaker
12. creator
13. prevention
14. highly
15. gladly

SKILL DRILL 3

A.
1. teacher
2. actor
3. baker
4. creator
5. player
6. prevention
7. speaker
8. worker

B.
9. gladly
10. highly
11. deeply
12. surely

C.
13. available
14. comfortable
15. dependable

SKILL DRILL 4

Order of answers may vary in 1–4, 5–9, 10–12, 13, 15.

1. deeply
2. highly
3. gladly
4. surely
5. baker
6. teacher
7. player
8. worker
9. speaker
10. available
11. dependable
12. comfortable
13. creation
14. prevention
15. action

WORD GAME 9

A pretzel is a *KNOT* of bread.

HOW WELL CAN YOU SPELL?

A.
1. highly
2. available
3. worker
4. player
5. surely
6. action
7. baker

B.
8. dependable
9. creation
10. prevention
11. speaker
12. comfortable
13. deeply
14. gladly
15. teacher

---

10. Popcorn Power

Pages 73–80

Objective

The purpose of this lesson is to review the previously taught uses of prefixes and suffixes and to introduce additional prefixes and suffixes. Special attention is placed on dissecting words to facilitate spelling and to help determine word meaning. In addition, the spelling rule concerning the suffix *ful* is demonstrated. (The only word in the English language that "ends" in *full* is "full.")

REVIEWING YOUR READING

1. b
2. c
3. d
4. a
5. a
6. d
7. b
8. d

FIGURING THE FACTS

1. T
2. F
3. T
4. T
5. T
6. F
7. T
8. T
9. T
10. T

WHAT'S YOUR OPINION?

Answers will vary.

SKILL DRILL 1

1. defense/ive
2. in/direct/ly
3. explos/ive
4. power/ful
5. wonder/ful
6. protect/ive
7. cheer/ful
8. un/grate/ful
9. inject/ion
10. un/event/ful
11. help/ful
12. predict/able
13. return/able
14. express/ive

SKILL DRILL 2

1. expressive
2. protective
3. explosive
4. promoter
5. returnable
6. uneventful
7. ungrateful
8. indirectly
9. injection
10. defensive
11. predictable

SKILL DRILL 3

1. helpful
2. predictable
3. promoter
4. returnable
5. expressive
6. cheerful
7. ungrateful
8. powerful
9. defensive
10. wonderful
11. indirectly
12. protective
13. explosive
14. uneventful
15. injection

SKILL DRILL 4

Order of answers may vary in 1–2, 3–4, 5–10, 11–12, 13–14.

1. expressive
2. explosive
3. indirectly
4. injection
5. cheerful
6. uneventful
7. helpful
8. ungrateful
9. powerful
10. wonderful
11. promoter
12. protective
13. predictable
14. returnable
15. defensive

WORD GAME 10

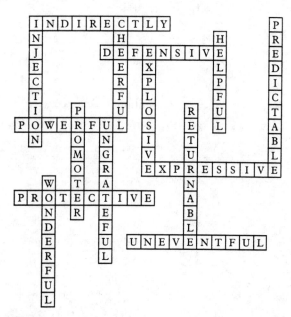

HOW WELL DO YOU SPELL?

A.
1. promoter
2. expressive
3. indirectly
4. powerful
5. predictable
6. uneventful
7. ungrateful

B.
8. wonderful
9. injection
10. cheerful
11. returnable
12. explosive
13. protective
14. helpful
15. defensive

11. Le Big Top

Pages 81–88

Objective

The teacher should note that the primary emphasis of this and of all the lessons in this book is on accurate spelling. In the next five lessons, we will focus on dividing words into syllables by identifying a pattern in the word. These patterns are merely an aid in syllabication, and should not be thought of as rules. Spelling research suggests that there is little value in committing patterns like these to memory as they do not always apply; however, we have made use of these patterns in *Spell It Out* to help the student examine the structure of the "Study List" words. The patterns are used strictly as a device to draw attention to the natural divisions in words and to facilitate spelling.

The examples used in "Developing Spelling Skills" are similar in structure to words previously studied in the book. The teacher should draw attention to the fact that prefixes, suffixes, and compounds are natural divisions in words, and are often syllables themselves.

REVIEWING YOUR READING

1. c   **2.** b   **3.** a   **4.** d   **5.** a   **6.** b   **7.** a   **8.** c

FIGURING THE FACTS

1. F   **2.** T   **3.** T   **4.** T   **5.** T   **6.** F   **7.** T   **8.** T   **9.** F
10. T

WHAT'S YOUR OPINION?

Answers will vary.

SKILL DRILL 1

1. fruit/cake	**2.** ad/vice	**3.** quar/ter	**4.** sin/cere	**5.** ex/pert
6. ac/tive	**7.** en/gine	**8.** cor/ner	**9.** al/most	**10.** pic/ture
11. cap/tain	**12.** in/side	**13.** vic/tim	**14.** doc/tor	**15.** sup/port

SKILL DRILL 2

1. fruit/cake	**2.** in/side	**3.** en/gine	**4.** doc/tor	**5.** ad/vice
6. ex/pert	**7.** sup/port	**8.** cap/tain	**9.** vic/tim	**10.** pic/ture
11. cor/ner	**12.** quar/ter	**13.** sin/cere	**14.** ac/tive	**15.** al/most

SKILL DRILL 3

1. doctor	**2.** picture	**3.** fruitcake	**4.** expert	**5.** advice
6. support	**7.** inside	**8.** victim	**9.** captain	**10.** corner
11. active	**12.** quarter	**13.** engine	**14.** sincere	

SKILL DRILL 4

1. engine	**2.** active	**3.** expert	**4.** quarter	**5.** advice
6. fruitcake	**7.** corner	**8.** victim	**9.** almost	**10.** doctor
11. captain	**12.** inside	**13.** support	**14.** picture	**15.** sincere

WORD GAME 11

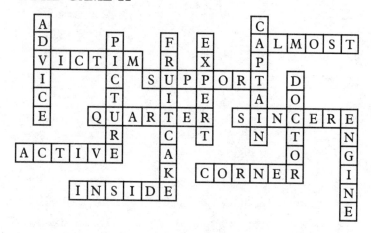

HOW WELL CAN YOU SPELL?

A. 1. support 2. inside 3. active 4. fruitcake 5. sincere

6. engine 7. victim

B. 8. advice 9. quarter 10. expert 11. corner 12. almost

13. picture 14. captain 15. doctor

---

12. Snakebite!

Pages 89–96

Objective

This lesson illustrates the use of the *vowel/consonant-vowel pattern* in certain words. As in the previous lesson, the "Study List" contains words that not only illustrate this pattern, but are similar in structure to those in preceding lessons, that is, compounds and words with prefixes. Once again, the emphasis here is on the natural division of sounds in words.

REVIEWING YOUR READING

1. c 2. d 3. a 4. c 5. b 6. d 7. b 8. c

FIGURING THE FACTS

1. F 2. T 3. F 4. F 5. T

Do not: 1. tie off the wound. 2. stop the flow of blood. 3. suck out the venom.

Do: 1. leave the bite alone. 2. keep the person calm. 3. relax yourself. 4. get the person to a doctor as soon as possible.

WHAT'S YOUR OPINION?

Answers will vary.

SKILL DRILL 1

1. re/call (v cv) 2. vo/cal (v cv) 3. wo/man (v cv) 4. to/day (v cv) 5. re/lax (v cv)

6. re/cent (v cv) 7. ma/jor (v cv) 8. sea/son (v cv) 9. de/light (v cv) 10. re/main (v cv)

11. ba/sis (v cv) 12. cri/sis (v cv) 13. poi/son (v cv) 14. va/por (v cv) 15. co/co/nut (v cv cv)

SKILL DRILL 2

1. remain	2. basis	3. today	4. vapor	5. season
6. vocal	7. crisis	8. poison	9. woman	10. delight
11. recall	12. relax	13. major	14. recent	15. coconut

SKILL DRILL 3

1. vocal	2. vapor	3. coconut	4. woman	5. delight
6. today	7. major			

SKILL DRILL 4

1. co/co/nut	2. re/lax	3. cri/sis	4. sea/son	5. va/por
6. re/main	7. vo/cal	8. re/cent	9. wo/man	10. de/light
11. ba/sis	12. ma/jor	13. poi/son	14. re/call	15. to/day

WORD GAME 12

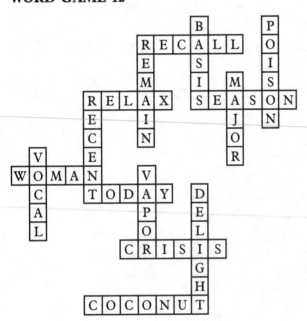

HOW WELL CAN YOU SPELL?

A.
1. delight	2. remain	3. recent	4. basis	5. major
6. vapor	7. crisis			

B.
8. relax	9. woman	10. today	11. poison	12. coconut
13. vocal	14. season	15. recall		

---

13. Computer Love

Pages 97–104

Objective

This lesson presents both the consonant-vowel/vowel-consonant pattern and the vowel/consonant-vowel pattern in the "Study List" words. The students are asked to identify the patterns and divide the words into syllables. This lesson also introduces the use of *y* as a vowel.

REVIEWING YOUR READING
1. b **2.** d **3.** b **4.** a **5.** a **6.** c **7.** b **8.** a

FIGURING THE FACTS
1. T **2.** T **3.** T **4.** T **5.** T **6.** F **7.** F **8.** T **9.** F
10. T

WHAT'S YOUR OPINION?
Answers will vary.

SKILL DRILL 1
1. fro/zen (v cv)   **2.** sher/bet (vc cv)   **3.** ne/ces/si/ty (v cvc vc vc)   **4.** se/lect (v cv)   **5.** spi/der (v cv)
6. mo/tion (v cv)   **7.** dif/fi/cult (vc cv cv)   **8.** des/sert (vc cv)   **9.** per/mit (vc cv)   **10.** sub/ject (cv vc)
11. no/ti/fy (v cv cv)   **12.** en/joy (vc cv)   **13.** fla/vor (v cv)   **14.** va/cant (v cv)   **15.** Tues/day (vc cv)

SKILL DRILL 2
1. Tuesday   **2.** flavor   **3.** motion   **4.** sherbet   **5.** necessity
6. difficult   **7.** select   **8.** vacant   **9.** spider   **10.** subject
11. notify   **12.** dessert   **13.** enjoy   **14.** permit   **15.** frozen

SKILL DRILL 3
1. Tuesday   **2.** vacant   **3.** difficult   **4.** flavor   **5.** spider
6. motion   **7.** notify   **8.** enjoy   **9.** select   **10.** subject
11. necessity   **12.** permit   **13.** frozen   **14.** dessert   **15.** sherbet

SKILL DRILL 4
Order of answers may vary in 1–6, 7–8, 9–10, 12–13, 14–15.

1. dessert   **2.** sherbet   **3.** permit   **4.** subject   **5.** select
6. vacant   **7.** difficult   **8.** notify   **9.** enjoy   **10.** Tuesday
11. necessity   **12.** frozen   **13.** motion   **14.** flavor   **15.** spider

WORD GAME 13

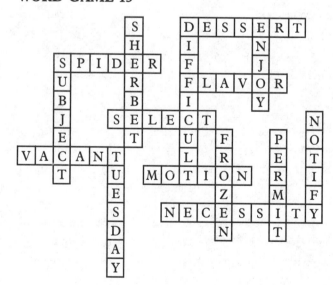

HOW WELL CAN YOU SPELL?

A. 1. frozen   2. sherbet   3. permit   4. vacant   5. select
   6. enjoy   7. difficult

B. 8. dessert   9. Tuesday   10. flavor   11. notify   12. necessity
   13. subject   14. spider   15. motion

---

14. Mechanical Music
Pages 105–112

Objective

This lesson continues the dissecting of words into syllables by introducing *consonant blends* to the process. The students are taught that consonant blends consist of two letters that perform as one by making only one sound. They are asked to integrate this concept with their knowledge of the syllabic patterns to divide words with consonant blends into syllables.

REVIEWING YOUR READING
1. d   2. a   3. c   4. d   5. d   6. d   7. b   8. b

FIGURING THE FACTS
1. T   2. T   3. F   4. F   5. T   6. F   7. T   8. T   9. T
10. T

WHAT'S YOUR OPINION?
Answers will vary.

SKILL DRILL 1
1. neu/tral (v cv)	2. den/tist (vc cv)	3. sur/prise (v c c v)	4. sand/wich (vc c v)	5. in/come (vc cv)
6. be/stow (v cv)	7. con/crete (vc cv)	8. ra/dio (v c v)	9. mu/sic (v cv)	10. bot/tom (vc cv)
11. in/ven/tor (vc c v c v)	12. pho/no/graph	13. in/stead (vc c v)	14. ar/gu/ment (vc cv cv)	15. ex/plore (vc cv)

SKILL DRILL 2
1. argument (dentist)	2. bestow (dentist, instead)	3. concrete	4. dentist (instead, bestow)	5. instead (bestow, dentist)
6. sandwich	7. neutral	8. phonograph	9. surprise	10. explore

SKILL DRILL 3
1. sandwich	2. concrete	3. inventor	4. phonograph	5. bestow
6. argument	7. explore	8. neutral	9. music	10. dentist
11. radio	12. income (instead)	13. bottom	14. instead (income)	15. surprise

SKILL DRILL 4
1. phonograph	2. music	3. dentist	4. explore	5. surprise
6. instead	7. bottom	8. concrete	9. bestow	10. neutral
11. inventor	12. radio	13. sandwich	14. income	15. argument

20

WORD GAME 14

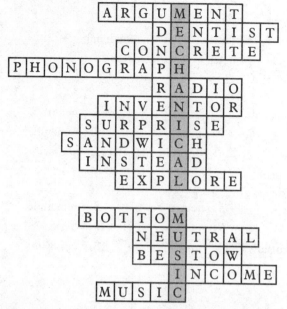

What does a player piano make? *MECHANICAL MUSIC*

HOW WELL CAN YOU SPELL?

A. 1. radio   2. neutral   3. income   4. bestow   5. phonograph

     6. bottom   7. sandwich

B. 8. dentist   9. argument   10. surprise   11. concrete   12. music

     13. inventor   14. explore   15. instead

---

15. King of Horror

Pages 113–120

Objective

     This is the final lesson dealing with syllabication. It therefore presents a review of all the previously learned concepts. Both the vowel/consonant/consonant-vowel and the vowel/consonant-vowel patterns are discussed. Longer and more difficult words that contain both patterns are examined at this point. Once again, the idea that not all words contain these patterns is emphasized. Students are urged to seek the natural syllabic divisions in words and to check the dictionary whenever in doubt.

REVIEWING YOUR READING

1. c   2. a   3. c   4. b   5. d   6. b   7. a   8. b

WHAT'S YOUR OPINION?

Answers will vary.

SKILL DRILL 1

1. your/self   2. im/mense   3. be/cause   4. pic/nic   5. sup/pose
6. ba/sic   7. v/men   8. op/po/site   9. his/to/ry   10. re/mem/ber
11. al/ways   12. be/gin   13. moun/tain/side   14. per/son   15. re/main/der

SKILL DRILL 2

Order of answers may vary in 1–3, 4–6, 7–11, 12–13.

1. always
2. person
3. picnic
4. because
5. immense
6. suppose
7. history
8. mountainside
9. opposite
10. remainder
11. remember
12. basic
13. begin
14. yourself
15. omen

SKILL DRILL 3

1. person
2. omen
3. mountainside
4. basic
5. begin
6. remainder
7. suppose
8. always
9. picnic
10. remember
11. because
12. history
13. immense
14. opposite
15. yourself

SKILL DRILL 4

1. yourself
2. person
3. suppose
4. remember
5. remainder
6. picnic
7. history
8. begin
9. because
10. basic
11. always
12. immense
13. mountainside
14. omen
15. opposite

WORD GAME 15

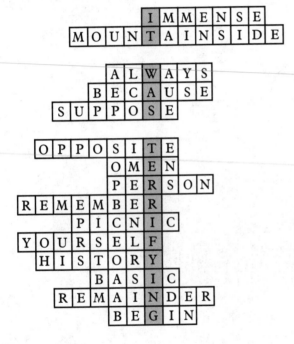

What could you say after reading a Stephen King book? *IT WAS TERRIFYING*

HOW WELL CAN YOU SPELL?

A.
1. yourself
2. because
3. remember
4. opposite
5. person
6. omen
7. remainder

B.
8. suppose
9. basic
10. begin
11. always
12. picnic
13. history
14. mountainside
15. immense

16. News Worthy

Pages 121–128

Objective

This lesson introduces words that contain *ei* or *ie*. The familiar *i before e* rule is explained and discussed. Students should commit this rule to memory as it is often helpful. The "Study List" words are representative of most words that contain this vowel combination. The teacher may wish to expand this "Study List" to include similar words that adhere to the rule, such as: *believe, brief, chief, conceit, deceit, deceive, frontier, grieve, handkerchief, mischief, niece, priest, relieve, shield,* and *thief.*

REVIEWING YOUR READING

1. c   **2.** d   **3.** b   **4.** d   **5.** a   **6.** b   **7.** d   **8.** b

FIGURING THE FACTS

1. T   **2.** F   **3.** T   **4.** F   **5.** T   **6.** T   **7.** F   **8.** T   **9.** F
10. F

WHAT'S YOUR OPINION?

Answers will vary.

SKILL DRILL 1

1. rel(ie)f   **2.** fr(ei)ght   **3.** p(ie)rce   **4.** f(ie)ld   **5.** n(ei)ghbor
6. c(ei)ling   **7.** sl(ei)gh   **8.** ach(ie)ve   **9.** bel(ie)f   **10.** rec(ei)pt
11. gr(ie)f   **12.** w(ei)gh   **13.** rec(ei)ve   **14.** r(ei)gn

SKILL DRILL 2

1. cashier   **2.** reign   **3.** receive   **4.** weigh   **5.** grief
6. belief   **7.** achieve   **8.** receipt   **9.** sleigh   **10.** ceiling
11. neighbor   **12.** pierce   **13.** freight   **14.** relief   **15.** field

SKILL DRILL 3

1. cashier   **2.** weigh   **3.** freight   **4.** belief   **5.** sleigh
6. achieve   **7.** neighbor   **8.** ceiling   **9.** receipt   **10.** reign
11. grief   **12.** receive   **13.** relief   **14.** pierce   **15.** field

SKILL DRILL 4

Order of answers may vary in 1–6, 8–10, 12–14.
1. achieve   **2.** belief   **3.** cashier   **4.** field   **5.** grief
6. pierce   **7.** relief   **8.** neighbor   **9.** reign   **10.** sleigh
11. weigh   **12.** ceiling   **13.** receipt   **14.** receive

WORD GAME 16

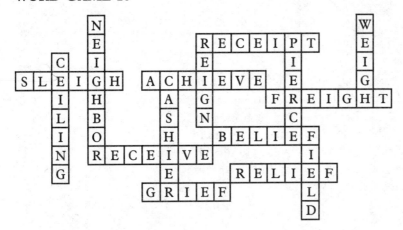

HOW WELL CAN YOU SPELL?

A. **1.** receive **2.** weigh **3.** pierce **4.** achieve **5.** belief

  6. freight **7.** reign

B. **8.** cashier **9.** field **10.** ceiling **11.** relief **12.** neighbor

  13. sleigh **14.** grief **15.** receipt

---

17. Sky People

Pages 129–136

Objective

    This lesson deals with the exceptions to the *i before e* rule. the "Study
List" contains the most common of these exceptions. Memorization of the
entire list is of little value as each of the individual words is an exception to
the rule for a particular reason. However, memorization of the individual
spellings is imperative. The best way for the student to become familiar with
the spellings is to use these words in his or her writing. The teacher should
assign work that stresses this type of practice.

REVIEWING YOUR READING

1. d **2.** d **3.** c **4.** b **5.** c **6.** a **7.** c **8.** b

FIGURING THE FACTS

1. T **2.** F **3.** F **4.** F **5.** T **6.** F **7.** T **8.** T **9.** F

10. T

WHAT'S YOUR OPINION?

Answers will vary.

SKILL DRILL 1

1. prot(ei)n **2.** l(ei)sure **3.** financ(ie)r **4.** w(ei)rd **5.** s(ei)zure

6. consc(ie)nce **7.** for(ei)gn **8.** n(ei)ther **9.** h(ei)ghts **10.** f(ie)ry

11. s(ei)ze **12.** sh(ei)k **13.** spec(ie)s **14.** (ei)ther **15.** anc(ie)nt

SKILL DRILL 2

1. species	2. protein	3. foreign	4. sheik	5. heights
6. fiery	7. leisure	8. conscience	9. ancient	10. financier
11. seizure	12. neither	13. weird	14. seize	15. either

SKILL DRILL 3

Order of answers may vary in 1–10, 11–15.

1. either	2. foreign	3. heights	4. leisure	5. neither
6. protein	7. seize	8. seizure	9. sheik	10. weird
11. ancient	12. conscience	13. fiery	14. financier	15. species

SKILL DRILL 4

1. seize	2. conscience	3. heights	4. either	5. leisure
6. ancient	7. protein	8. neither	9. sheik	10. financier
11. foreign	12. weird	13. species	14. fiery	15. seizure

WORD GAME 17

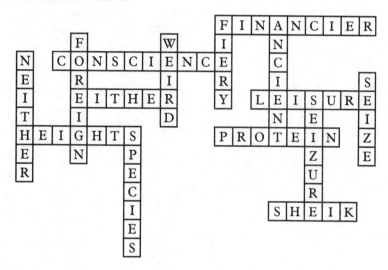

HOW WELL CAN YOU SPELL?

A.

1. fiery	2. ancient	3. neither	4. seize	5. weird
6. seizure	7. financier	8. species		

B.

9. protein	10. foreign	11. leisure	12. height	13. sheik
14. Either	15. conscience			

---

18. Our Friends With Flippers

Pages 137–144

Objective

This rule for the formation of plurals in words that end with *y* is taught in this lesson and in Lesson 19. The first half of the rule is explained here. When a word ends in *y* preceded by a vowel, we simply add *s* to the end of the word. All of the "Study List" words end with the vowel *y* and form their plurals according to this rule.

REVIEWING YOUR READING
1. c **2.** c **3.** a **4.** a **5.** d **6.** b **7.** d **8.** b

FIGURING THE FACTS
1. F **2.** T **3.** T **4.** F **5.** F **6.** T **7.** F **8.** T **9.** T
10. T

WHAT'S YOUR OPINION?
Answers will vary.

SKILL DRILL 1
1. surv(ey)	**2.** attorn(ey)	**3.** monk(ey)	**4.** ess(ay)	**5.** birthd(ay)
6. turk(ey)	**7.** vall(ey)	**8.** holid(ay)	**9.** journ(ey)	**10.** bu(oy)
11. weekd(ay)	**12.** all(ey)	**13.** displ(ay)	**14.** chimn(ey)	**15.** donk(ey)

SKILL DRILL 2
1. alleys	**2.** buoys	**3.** donkeys	**4.** birthdays	**5.** journeys
6. displays	**7.** weekdays	**8.** attorneys	**9.** chimneys	**10.** essays
11. holidays	**12.** monkeys	**13.** surveys	**14.** turkeys	**15.** valleys

SKILL DRILL 3
1. donkey	**2.** birthday	**3.** display	**4.** journey	**5.** valley
6. chimney	**7.** monkey	**8.** weekday	**9.** alley	**10.** buoy
11. holiday	**12.** turkey	**13.** essay	**14.** attorney	**15.** survey

SKILL DRILL 4
Order of answers may vary in 1–5, 7–15.
1. birthday	**2.** display	**3.** essay	**4.** holiday	**5.** weekday
6. buoy	**7.** alley	**8.** attorney	**9.** chimney	**10.** donkey
11. journey	**12.** monkey	**13.** survey	**14.** turkey	**15.** valley

WORD GAME 18

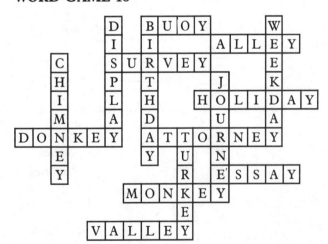

HOW WELL CAN YOU SPELL?

A.
1. birthday   2. holiday   3. monkey   4. weekday   5. buoy
6. chimneys   7. displays

B.
8. valley   9. turkey   10. essay   11. survey   12. donkey
13. journey   14. alley   15. attorney

---

19. Opera Star

Pages 145–152

Objective

The second half of the rule dealing with pluralization of words ending in *y* is explained in this lesson. When a word ends in *y* preceded by a consonant, we change the *y* to *i* and add *es* when forming the plural. All of the "Study List" words adhere to this rule. The teacher should take this opportunity to compare the "Study Lists" of Lessons 18 and 19 in order to ensure that the students become aware of both aspects of the rule (*y* preceded by a consonant and *y* preceded by a vowel).

Once again it should be stated that memorization of the rule may be of little use to the student in the future. The rule should be looked upon only as a tool that will help familiarize the student with patterns in English spelling. In this way, the student will eventually develop a "spelling intuitiveness," which will naturally lead him or her to correct spelling choices.

REVIEWING YOUR READING

1. b   2. d   3. a   4. d   5. a   6. c   7. b   8. a

FIGURING THE FACTS

1. T   2. F   3. T   4. T   5. T   6. T   7. F   8. T   9. T
10. T

WHAT'S YOUR OPINION?

Answers will vary.

SKILL DRILL 1

1. ju(ry)   2. abili(ty)   3. libra(ry)   4. trea(ty)   5. facto(ry)
6. varie(ty)   7. centu(ry)   8. po(ny)   9. poli(cy)   10. count(ry)
11. fami(ly)   12. ci(ty)   13. dia(ry)   14. victo(ry)   15. compa(ny)

SKILL DRILL 2

1. abilities   2. cities   3. countries   4. juries   5. libraries
6. ponies   7. treaties   8. centuries   9. companies   10. diaries
11. factories   12. policies   13. families   14. varieties   15. victories

SKILL DRILL 3

1. jury	2. library	3. pony	4. company	5. diary
6. century	7. treaty	8. family	9. policy	10. factory
11. country	12. ability	13. city	14. variety	15. victory

SKILL DRILL 4

1. cities	2. company	3. ponies	4. jury	5. family
6. policy	7. ability	8. centuries	9. countries	10. treaty
11. factory	12. library	13. diary	14. victory	15. variety

WORD GAME 19

Where is Kathleen Battle the star? In the *OPERA*

HOW WELL CAN YOU SPELL?

A. 1. libraries 2. companies 3. factories 4. abilities 5. variety

6. treaties 7. policies 8. centuries

B. 9. countries 10. victories 11. juries 12. ponies 13. diary

14. cities 15. family

---

20. Veins of Fire

Pages 153–160

Objective

This lesson introduces some of the most commonly misspelled words in the English language. Here the teacher should encourage the use of mnemonics. The emphasis here should be on the student's careful examination of the spelling of each word. If the student makes mental notes of what is odd or unusual about the spelling of each word before actually beginning to learn and use the word in writing, he or she will be more apt to remember the unusual spelling. Once again, the emphasis here should be on encouraging the students to use the words in their writing.

REVIEWING YOUR READING

1. a 2. b 3. d 4. c 5. a 6. b 7. a 8. c

FIGURING THE FACTS

1. T 2. T 3. F 4. T 5. F 6. T 7. F 8. T 9. T
10. T

WHAT'S YOUR OPINION?

Answers will vary.

SKILL DRILL 1

1. e(qu)ipment	2. ic(i)cle	3. (h)eir	4. mi(s)er	5. clo(th)es
6. appear(a)nce	7. bu(s)y	8. fert(i)le	9. Feb(r)uary	10. lab(or)at(or)y
11. oa(s)is	12. val(ua)ble	13. ben(e)fit	14. cel(e)ry	15. (e)m(e)rg(e)ncy

SKILL DRILL 2

1. clothes	2. benefit	3. laboratory	4. appearance	5. miser
6. fertile	7. celery	8. valuable	9. emergency	10. equipment
11. icicle	12. hair	13. oasis	14. February	15. busy

SKILL DRILL 3

1. equipment	2. laboratory	3. appearance	4. emergency	5. benefit
6. valuable	7. clothes	8. busy	9. February	10. celery
11. oasis	12. heir	13. fertile	14. miser	15. icicle

SKILL DRILL 4

1. busy	2. valuable	3. clothes	4. emergency	5. benefit
6. laboratory	7. February	8. heir	9. oasis	10. Celery
11. equipment	12. miser	13. icicle	14. fertile	15. appearance

WORD GAME 20

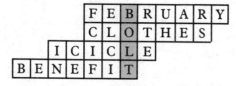

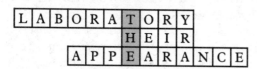

What is another name for lightning? *BOLT FROM THE BLUE*

HOW WELL CAN YOU SPELL?

A.
| 1. celery | 2. oasis | 3. appearance | 4. emergency | 5. busy |
| 6. miser | 7. February | | | |

B.
| 8. clothes | 9. valuable | 10. benefit | 11. laboratory | 12. heir |
| 13. icicle | 14. fertile | 15. equipment | | |

Spell It Out—Book 2
Sample Lesson Plan

Professional Talkers
Pages 1–8

Objectives
• To learn the rule: When a word ends with a single consonant, double the consonant when adding a suffix that begins with a vowel.

• To improve the reading skills by finding the main idea, remembering details, making inferences through experience and exercises.

Motivation
For this lesson, you might want to ask students to discuss any Arsenio Hall Show episode that they may have seen. Ask them to talk about what guests they saw on that particular show, and why they enjoyed those guests. Discuss Arsenio Hall's popularity and elicit students' responses about why they like him.

Procedure
1. Have the students survey the opening picture. Ask questions about the picture. Who is in the picture? What is he doing? Why do you think the selection is titled "Professional Talker"?

2. Have students read the story silently. Instruct them to turn the page and complete the "Reviewing Your Reading" and the "Figuring the Facts" exercises.

3. Choose students to go back and read the story aloud. Then ask individual students to read and answer the questions orally. This will provide a group activity and an answer check for all students.

4. Direct the students to answer the "What's Your Opinion?" exercise. This exercise may be used as a discussion activity, a writing activity, or both. Students may write their answers, then read them aloud. They may also discuss the differences in their answers. Since the students' answers will vary, they will not appear in the answer key that follows.

5. Have students turn to the section entitled "Developing Spelling Skills." Explain that the words in dark type appear in the reading selection and that they demonstrate a particular pattern that applies to a spelling rule. The text will help you to explain the rule and its uses. Your demonstration should include a review of consonants and vowels. It would also be wise to review all the meanings of the "Study List" words with the class and instruct students to refer to the "Mini-Dictionary" (page 162) to find the definitions they are unsure of.

6. Direct the students to begin the series of "Skill Drills." The answers to the "Skill Drills" have been arranged in alphabetical order, where applicable, for your convenience. In "Skill Drill 3," for example, the students are asked to list the words from the "Study List" that contain a double *p* and end with the suffix *ed*. Although the student may list the words in any order, the *Answer Key* will list the words alphabetically.

7. After the four "Skill Drills" and the "Word Game" have been completed and checked, direct the students to do "How Well Can You Spell?" a review quiz. You might want to have the students check their own work while you read the correct answers.

Follow Up
1. Have the students do research in recent periodicals on Arsenio Hall, or other talk show hosts and prepare a short written or oral report.

2. Ask students to make a list of one-syllable words that end in a single consonant. Then have students exchange lists and add the endings *ed*, *est*, and *ing* to the words they have found. Remind students to be sure that the base word is actually still a word after adding the ending. For example, the word *hit* becomes *hitter* and *hitting* but *not hittest*. Explain that the three endings cannot be added to every word.

3. The traditional spelling bee is a good reinforcement for a spelling lesson. The most common type is the two-team competition, but some variations on the theme may increase student interest and participation.

4. Follow every few lessons with a test. Say each word once, use each word in a sentence, then say each word again. Students should not begin writing until you have completed the sequence.

Guide and Answer Key

---

1. Professional Talker

Pages 1–8

Objectives

This lesson focuses on the first part of the doubling rule and should be considered a prerequisite to the next four chapters that also deal with the doubling of consonants. Because there are no auditory clues to distinguish the single *k* of *walked* from the double *p* of *stopped* it is imperative that spelling be based on a visual perception of the word along with memorization and application of a particular rule. The "Skill Drills" and "Word Game" reinforce this type of learning by asking students to write words ending in a single consonant and then later to double that consonant as application of the rule is called for. The ultimate aim of this and other lessons is to provide the student with a rule that is applicable to hundreds of other words, thus reducing his or her need to memorize and increasing the ability to transfer knowledge.

REVIEWING YOUR READING

1. a   **2.** c   **3.** b   **4.** c   **5.** c   **6.** b   **7.** a   **8.** b

FIGURING THE FACTS

1. F   **2.** F   **3.** F   **4.** T   **5.** F   **6.** T   **7.** F   **8.** T   **9.** F
10. T

WHAT'S YOUR OPINION?

Answers will vary.

SKILL DRILL 1

1. ru(nn)er	**2.** sla(pp)ed	**3.** spli(tt)ing	**4.** tra(pp)ed	**5.** bi(gg)est
6. dro(pp)ed	**7.** fi(tt)ing	**8.** shi(pp)ing	**9.** sli(pp)ed	**10.** sto(pp)ed
11. wi(nn)er	**12.** cla(pp)ing	**13.** fa(nn)ed	**14.** hi tt er	**15.** pla(nn)ed

SKILL DRILL 2

1. biggest	**2.** winner	**3.** trapped	**4.** stopped	**5.** splitting
6. slipped	**7.** fanned	**8.** dropped	**9.** clapping	**10.** slapped
11. shipping	**12.** runner	**13.** fitting	**14.** hitter	**15.** planned

SKILL DRILL 3

Order of answers may vary in 1–5, 6–7, 8–9, 11–12, 14–15.

1. dropped	**2.** slapped	**3.** slipped	**4.** stopped	**5.** trapped
6. fanned	**7.** planned	**8.** fitting	**9.** splitting	**10.** biggest
11. clapping	**12.** shipping	**13.** hitter	**14.** runner	**15.** winner

SKILL DRILL 4

1. winner	2. runner	3. stopped	4. biggest	5. fanned
6. trapped	7. clapping	8. dropped	9. planned	10. fitting
11. hitter	12. slipped	13. splitting	14. shipping	15. slapped

WORD GAME 1

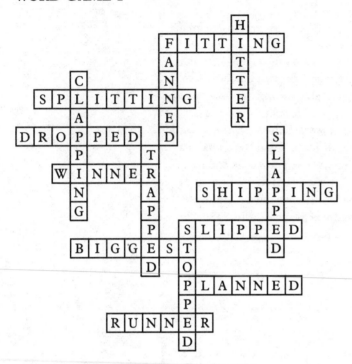

HOW WELL CAN YOU SPELL?

A.

1. splitting	2. hitter	3. planned	4. clapping	5. trapped
6. fanned	7. fitting			

B.

8. shipping	9. slipped	10. biggest	11. winner	12. stopped
13. runner	14. slapped	15. dropped		

An Additional Activity

Have the students use the suffixes *est*, *ed*, *er*, and *ing* to create new words from the "Study List." For example *biggest* can be changed to *bigger*, *fitting* can be changed to *fitted*, or *fittest*, etc.

Supplementary Words

Lesson 1

banner	betted	fatter	tapping
barred	bitter	flapped	tarred
batted	capped	hidden	tipped
bedding	cutting	rubber	wagged

2. Flying Saucers

Pages 9–16

Objective

In this lesson students study a rule that is actually an exception to the doubling rule. The main objective of the lesson is for students to be able to add a suffix to a word by quickly differentiating between the consonants and vowels at the end of a word, which determine whether the final consonant is doubled. Since there are no sound-spelling correlations to help determine the proper ending, it is important that pupils internalize this rule by looking at a word, mentally identifying the last two letters, and then making a decision as to whether to double the final consonant or leave it alone.

Before beginning the exercises, attention should be given to a review of the consonants and also the last two letters of each word in the "Study List" for help in mastering this spelling rule.

REVIEWING YOUR READING

1. b   **2.** b   **3.** d   **4.** c   **5.** d   **6.** c   **7.** b   **8.** b

FIGURING THE FACTS

1. T   **2.** T   **3.** T   **4.** T   **5.** F   **6.** T   **7.** T   **8.** F   **9.** F
10. T

WHAT'S YOUR OPINION?

Answers will vary.

SKILL DRILL 1

1. walk(ing)	**2.** thank(ed)	**3.** stack(ed)	**4.** rent(ed)	**5.** pack(ed)
6. jump(ing)	**7.** farm(er)	**8.** think(ing)	**9.** stand(ing)	**10.** shrink(ing)
11. pitch(ing)	**12.** lift(ed)	**13.** hunt(er)	**14.** earn(ing)	**15.** catch(ing)

SKILL DRILL 2

1. hunter	**2.** stacked	**3.** standing	**4.** thanked	**5.** catching
6. thinking	**7.** lifted	**8.** packed	**9.** jumping	**10.** earning
11. walking	**12.** shrinking	**13.** farmer	**14.** pitching	**15.** rented

SKILL DRILL 3

Order of answers may vary in 1–2, 3–7, 8–9, 10–11.

1. farmer	**2.** hunter	**3.** lifted	**4.** packed	**5.** rented
6. stacked	**7.** thanked	**8.** shrinking	**9.** thinking	**10.** catching
11. pitching	**12.** walking	**13.** earning	**14.** jumping	**15.** standing

SKILL DRILL 4

1. pitching   2. farmer   3. packed   4. rented   5. hunter

6. jumping   7. lifted   8. shrinking   9. thanked   10. thinking

11. earning   12. walking   13. stacked   14. standing   15. catching

WORD GAME 2

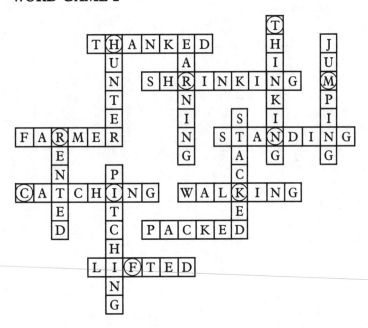

HOW WELL CAN YOU SPELL?

A.   1. farmer   2. stacked   3. shrinking   4. hunter   5. thinking

     6. walking   7. jumping

B.   8. earning   9. packed   10. rented   11. standing   12. catching

     13. lifted   14. thanked   15. pitching

Additional Activities

As in Lesson 1, have students alternate suffixes from word to word. Change *catching* to *catcher,* *earning* to *earned,* etc.

Call out different letters of the alphabet and ask students to identify them as vowels or consonants. You might also ask students to write out their complete name and count the number of vowels and consonants.

Supplementary Words

Lesson 2

backed	doubting	pumped
blacked	dumping	punting
blinking	learned	shifted
burned	linking	sinking
charmer	lumping	stinking

3. Write On!

Pages 17–24

Objective

In this lesson the student is presented with another rule that emphasizes when a final consonant is NOT doubled. The attention given to a review of vowels and consonants in Lesson 2 should be repeated in this lesson. The word *preceded* is used in the definition and is a key to the understanding of this spelling rule. The visual and oral explanations listed in "An Additional Activity" may prove helpful to students in establishing a concrete definition for the word.

REVIEWING YOUR READING

1. b　　**2.** c　　**3.** c　　**4.** b　　**5.** a　　**6.** c　　**7.** d　　**8.** a

FIGURING THE FACTS

1. T　　**2.** F　　**3.** T　　**4.** T　　**5.** T　　**6.** F　　**7.** T　　**8.** F　　**9.** T
10. T

WHAT'S YOUR OPINION?

Answers will vary.

SKILL DRILL 1

1. speak(ing)　　**2.** need(ed)　　**3.** read(ing)　　**4.** mean(ing)　　**5.** look(ing)
6. hear(ing)　　**7.** feel(ing)　　**8.** seal(ed)　　**9.** sail(ing)　　**10.** meet(ing)
11. lean(ing)　　**12.** kneel(ing)　　**13.** heal(ed)　　**14.** fail(ed)　　**15.** clean(ed)

SKILL DRILL 2

1. looking　　**2.** leaning　　**3.** failed　　**4.** meaning　　**5.** cleaned
6. meeting　　**7.** reading　　**8.** needed　　**9.** sailing　　**10.** feeling
11. sealed　　**12.** hearing　　**13.** healed　　**14.** kneeling　　**15.** speaking

SKILL DRILL 3

Order of answers may vary in 1–5, 6–8, 10–11, 13–15.

1. hearing　　**2.** leaning　　**3.** meaning　　**4.** reading　　**5.** speaking
6. feeling　　**7.** kneeling　　**8.** meeting　　**9.** looking　　**10.** failed
11. sailing　　**12.** needed　　**13.** cleaned　　**14.** healed　　**15.** sealed

SKILL DRILL 4

1. sealed　　**2.** leaning　　**3.** speaking　　**4.** sailing　　**5.** reading
6. needed　　**7.** meeting　　**8.** meaning　　**9.** kneeling　　**10.** hearing
11. healed　　**12.** looking　　**13.** feeling　　**14.** failed　　**15.** cleaned

WORD GAME 3

What does John Irving do best? *WRITE*

HOW WELL CAN YOU SPELL?

A. 1. kneeling   2. feeling   3. meaning   4. reading   5. hearing
     6. sailing   7. needed

B. 8. speaking   9. healed   10. failed   11. sealed   12. meeting
    13. cleaned   14. leaning   15. needed

An Additional Activity

Explain the word *preceded* by lining up a few students and ask which student precedes another or ask pupils to name the two months that precede March or the two numbers that precede eight.

All of the suffixes used in this lesson are either *ing* or *ed*. Therefore, it will be easy for students to substitute suffixes from word to word. Make students aware of the irregular changes such as *feeling* to *felt*, *hearing* to *heard*, *kneeling* to *knelt*, *meeting* to *met*, *reading* to *read*, *speaking* to *spoke*.

Supplementary Words

Lesson 3

bailed	leaned	seemed
clearing	mailed	wailing
feeding	meaning	weakened
gained	sailed	
hailed	sealing	

---

4. Hello, Dolly

Pages 25–32

Objective

This lesson presents all three rules concerned with doubling a final consonant. At this point you should make your students aware of the relationship of all three rules. All of them deal with words that end in consonants, and add syllables that begin with vowels. The general rule is the following: If there is only one final consonant, double it. If there are two final consonants, leave them alone. If there is one consonant preceded by two vowels, leave it alone. While some students may put these facts together on their own, it is advised that you help the students make the connection.

REVIEWING YOUR READING

1. d   2. b   3. a   4. c   5. d   6. b   7. b   8. c

FIGURING THE FACTS

1. F   2. T   3. F   4. F   5. F   6. T   7. T   8. F   9. F
10. T

WHAT'S YOUR OPINION?

Answers will vary.

SKILL DRILL 1

1. plead(ing)
2. check(ing)
3. sign(ing)
4. skimm(ed)
5. want(ed)
6. talk(ing)
7. faint(ing)
8. jogg(ing)
9. sing(ing)
10. paint(ed)
11. wrapp(ed)
12. trimm(ed)
13. fool(ing)
14. dream(ing)
15. beginn(er)

SKILL DRILL 2

1. painted
2. signing
3. fooling
4. talking
5. beginner
6. trimmed
7. wanted
8. dreaming
9. fainting
10. wrapped
11. singing
12. checking
13. jogging
14. skimmed
15. pleading

SKILL DRILL 3

Order of answers may vary in 1–5, 6–7, 9–10, 12–13.

1. beginner
2. jogging
3. skimmed
4. trimmed
5. wrapped
6. fainting
7. painted
8. fooling
9. dreaming
10. pleading
11. wanted or fainting
12. signing
13. singing
14. talking
15. checking

SKILL DRILL 4

1. beginner
2. wrapped
3. wanted
4. jogging
5. fooling
6. fainting
7. dreaming
8. checking
9. trimmed
10. talking
11. singing
12. pleading
13. skimmed
14. signing
15. painted

WORD GAME 4

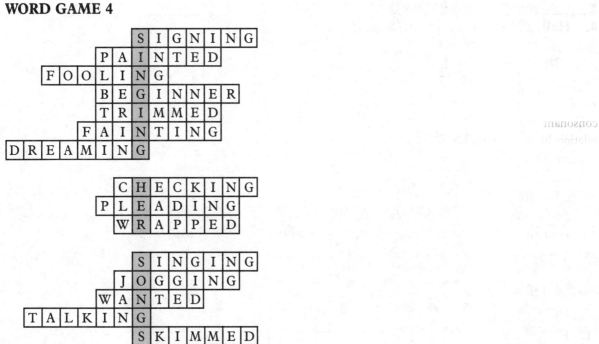

What does Dolly Parton enjoy doing most? *SINGING HER SONGS*

HOW WELL CAN YOU SPELL?

A.
1. pleading
2. fainting
3. beginner
4. skimmed
5. checking
6. trimmed
7. daydreaming
8. painted

B.
9. talking
10. Signing
11. wanted
12. jogging
13. wrapped
14. fooling
15. singing

An Additional Activity

To reinforce these three rules write out words from Lessons 1, 2, and 3 on slips of paper. Divide the class into teams. Ask each student to take a word. Give students time to read the word, decide which rule applies and why, and then explain their answer to their classmates. Record points for each correct answer. The team with the most points wins.

Supplementary Words

Lesson 4

Refer to "Supplementary Words" for Lesson 3

---

5. Holes in Space

Pages 33–40

Objective

In conjunction with Lesson 4, this lesson deals with a review of the three rules concerning doubling of a final consonant. Again, emphasize the relationship of the three rules. Students may be more apt to remember the rules if they credit themselves for finding the "key" to the rule. Of course, this would depend upon individual teaching methods.

REVIEWING YOUR READING

1. c   **2.** c   **3.** b   **4.** b   **5.** b   **6.** a   **7.** d   **8.** b

FIGURING THE FACTS

1. T   **2.** T   **3.** T   **4.** F   **5.** T   **6.** T   **7.** T   **8.** T   **9.** F
10. T

WHAT'S YOUR OPINION?

Answers will vary.

SKILL DRILL 1

1. preferr(ed)	**2.** accept(ed)	**3.** enlist(ed)	**4.** appear(ed)	**5.** contain(ed)
6. clear(ed)	**7.** result(ing)	**8.** permitt(ed)	**9.** collect(ing)	**10.** cash(ed)
11. seat(ed)	**12.** forgett(ing)	**13.** omitt(ed)	**14.** spinn(ing)	**15.** suit(able)

SKILL DRILL 2

1. cleared	**2.** enlisted	**3.** accepted	**4.** omitted	**5.** contained
6. collecting	**7.** suitable	**8.** seated	**9.** forgetting	**10.** appeared
11. resulting	**12.** spinning	**13.** cashed	**14.** permitted	**15.** preferred

SKILL DRILL 3

Order of answers may vary in 1–8.

1. accepted	**2.** appeared	**3.** collecting	**4.** forgetting	**5.** omitted
6. permitted	**7.** preferred	**8.** spinning	**9.** enlisted	**10.** cashed
11. cleared	**12.** seated	**13.** suitable	**14.** resulting	**15.** contained

SKILL DRILL 4

1. contained	2. resulting	3. suitable	4. cleared	5. seated
6. cashed	7. enlisted	8. spinning	9. collecting	10. accepted
11. preferred	12. appeared	13. permitted	14. forgetting	15. omitted

WORD GAME 5

HOW WELL CAN YOU SPELL?

A.
1. resulting	2. suitable	3. enlisted	4. spinning	5. accepted
6. preferred	7. permitted	8. cashed		

B.
9. contained	10. seated	11. appeared	12. forgetting	13. collecting
14. cleared	15. omitted			

An Additional Activity

Have students prepare two sets of "flash cards," one with the words from the first five lessons, minus the suffixes, the other with the suffixes. Ask students to test each other by holding up one of each set, side by side, and deciding whether they should double the final consonant or not. Then have students spell the new word correctly.

Supplementary Words

Lesson 5

Refer to "Supplementary Words" for Lesson 3.

Optional Testing List

Lessons 1-5

accepted	hitter	seated
appeared	hunter	shipping
beginner	jogging	shrinking
biggest	jumping	signing
cashed	kneeling	singing
catching	leaking	skimmed
checking	leaning	slapped
clapping	lifted	slipped
cleaned	meaning	speaking
cleared	meeting	spinning
collecting	needed	splitting
contained	omitted	stacked
dreaming	packed	standing
dropped	painted	stopped
earning	permitted	suitable
enlisted	pitching	talking
failed	planned	thanked
fainting	pleading	thinking
fanned	preferred	trapped
farmer	reading	trimmed
feeling	rented	walking
fooling	resulting	wanted
forgetting	runner	winner
healed	sailing	wrapped
hearing	sealed	

6. About Scouts

Pages 41-48

Objective

This lesson deals with the *ou* sound and its many variations. The absence of a phonetic spelling for each word forces the student to make letter-sound correspondences in terms of the whole word as opposed to individual letters. The sound clues of *ou* in *foundation* and the *ou* in *would* do not resemble one another when looked at within the context of the other letters in the word. This whole-word approach should be emphasized by reviewing the pronunciation of the "Study List" words because we are dealing with similar spellings of different sounds.

REVIEWING YOUR READING

1. b   2. c   3. c   4. c   5. b   6. a   7. b   8. d

FIGURING THE FACTS

1. T   2. T   3. T   4. F; Girl Scout Troop   5. T   6. T   7. T   8. T
9. T   10. F; 18

WHAT'S YOUR OPINION?

Answers will vary.

SKILL DRILL 1

1. sh(ou)lder	2. c(ou)ntry	3. b(ou)lder	4. acc(ou)nt	5. bl(ou)se
6. p(ou)nd	7. c(ou)rte(ou)s	8. c(ou)nter	9. b(ou)ndary	10. ast(ou)nd
11. b(ou)nce	12. c(ou)ld	13. f(ou)ndation	14. w(ou)ld	15. t(ou)rist

SKILL DRILL 2

1. foundation	2. counter	3. boulder	4. astound	5. bounce
6. blouse	7. boundary	8. tourist	9. could	10. country
11. courteous	12. account	13. shoulder	14. would	15. pound

SKILL DRILL 3

1. would	2. account	3. country	4. boundary	5. foundation
6. boulder	7. astound	8. courteous	9. shoulder	10. could
11. tourist	12. counter	13. bounce	14. blouse	15. pound

SKILL DRILL 4

Order of answers may vary in 2–4, 6–7, 9–10, 11–12.

1. courteous	2. would	3. could	4. pound	5. shoulder
6. blouse	7. bounce	8. foundation	9. boulder	10. counter
11. account	12. tourist			

WORD GAME 6

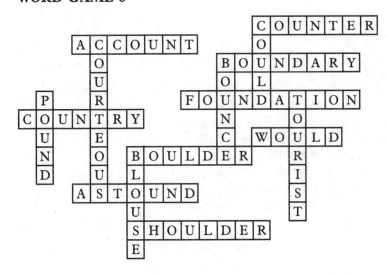

HOW WELL CAN YOU SPELL?

A. **1.** boulder **2.** blouse **3.** boundary **4.** pound **5.** courteous

  6. tourist **7.** astound

B. **8.** could **9.** would **10.** country **11.** counter **12.** account

  13. shoulder **14.** bounce **15.** foundation

An Additional Activity

Have students clip an article out of a daily newspaper and mount it on a piece of cardboard. (The purpose of the cardboard is to enable students to use this same article in the upcoming weeks.) Have students look for words that contain the *ou* vowel combination and circle them. Keep a chart in the classroom that lists how many times the combination has been found by each student. Leave space so that scores may be kept for finding the patterns for words in the upcoming chapters. Make it a competition for a prize or a special grade.

Supplementary Words

Lesson 6

about	house	ought
amount	loud	ounce
found	mountain	pour
fountain	mouse	rough
ground	noun	sound
hound	ouch	sour

7. Sails Away!

Pages 49–56

Objective

In this lesson pupils are asked to become familiar with the long *i* sound spelled with a *y*. The words in the "Study List" demonstrate the various ways that *y* is used to make the long *i* sound. The unusual spelling should be mentioned to students in an attempt to help them realize that sound representations are not always accurate. Quite often a word is not spelled the way it sounds in spoken language. Pronunciation of all "Study List" words should be reviewed because the only way a student will know the long *i* sound of *myself* from the short *i* sound of *syllable* is to pronounce the entire word, write it several times, and then see it often in print. There is no consistency of language to be offered in this case, and that fact should be explained when one- and two-syllable words that look quite simple become very difficult.

REVIEWING YOUR READING

1. d **2.** c **3.** a **4.** b **5.** c **6.** d **7.** b **8.** c

FIGURING THE FACTS

1. T **2.** F **3.** T **4.** T **5.** T **6.** T **7.** F **8.** T **9.** T

10. F

WHAT'S YOUR OPINION?

Answers will vary.

SKILL DRILL 1

1. n(y)lon	2. h(y)drant	3. t(y)rant	4. as(y)lum	5. d(y)namic
6. h(y)giene	7. paral(y)ze	8. e(y)elid	9. t(y)pewriter	10. c(y)clone
11. pl(y)wood	12. d(y)namite	13. m(y)self	14. rec(y)cle	15. st(y)le

SKILL DRILL 2

1. typewriter	2. hydrant	3. eyelid	4. nylon	5. style
6. myself	7. hygiene	8. dynamite	9. dynamic	10. recycle
11. cyclone	12. paralyze	13. asylum	14. plywood	15. tyrant

SKILL DRILL 3

1. myself	2. tyrant	3. style	4. typewriter	5. plywood
6. eyelid	7. dynamic	8. dynamite	9. paralyze	10. hygiene
11. asylum	12. nylon	13. hydrant	14. recycle	15. cyclone

SKILL DRILL 4

Order of answers may vary in 1–2, 3–6, 8–10.

1. nylon	2. style	3. cycle	4. dynamic	5. hydrant
6. hygiene	7. typewriter	8. eyelid	9. myself	10. tyrant
11. dynamite and paralyze	12. recycle	13. asylum	14. plywood	15. eyelid, myself, and typewriter

WORD GAME 7

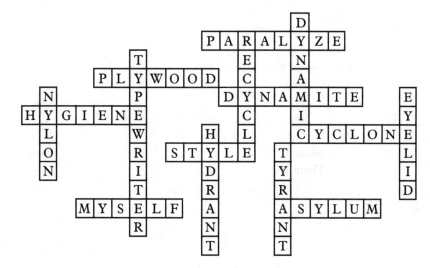

HOW WELL CAN YOU SPELL?

A. 1. style   2. hygiene   3. tyrant   4. asylum   5. paralyze

6. plywood   7. cyclone

B. 8. recycle   9. dynamic   10. hydrant   11. eyelid   12. nylon

13. dynamite   14. myself   15. typewriter

An Additional Activity

Divide the class into several groups. Explain that their assignment is to find as many words as possible that contain the long *i*. Ask one member of the group to record answers. After ten or fifteen minutes, have one student in each group read the answers aloud while you write them on the blackboard. The winner is the group with the most words containing the long *i*. While writing out the words point out any words containing the *i* sound spelled with a *y*.

Supplementary Words

Lesson 7

bye	rye
cycle	tying
dye	typhoid
hydrogen	python
lying	xylophone

8. Artist and Architect

Pages 57–64

Objective

As in the previous lessons, it is most important for the teacher to review the pronunciation of the "Study List" words for the students. Contrast the short *i* sounds with the long *i* sounds that appeared in the previous lesson.

These are several words in this lesson that contain two *y*'s. The teacher should make the student aware of this and point out that except for the word *synonym*, the short *i* sound appears only once in these words.

REVIEWING YOUR READING

1. b   2. d   3. b   4. b   5. c   6. a   7. a   8. a

FIGURING THE FACTS

1. T   2. T   3. F; very little   4. T   5. F; 1955   6. T
7. F; a record of events   8. T   9. F; Alabama   10. T

WHAT'S YOUR OPINION?

Answers will vary.

SKILL DRILL 1

1. h(y)pnotize
2. s(y)mpathy
3. s(y)rup
4. s(y)mptom
5. m(y)stery
6. m(y)thology
7. cr y stal
8. l y rics
9. s(y)non(y)m
10. s(y)stem
11. t(y)pical
12. m(y)th
13. s(y)llable
14. p(y)ramid
15. s(y)mbol

SKILL DRILL 2

1. mythology
2. mystery
3. symbol
4. crystal
5. system
6. synonym
7. hypnotize
8. myth
9. typical
10. pyramid
11. syllable
12. syrup
13. lyrics
14. sympathy
15. symptom

SKILL DRILL 3

1. crystal
2. pyramid
3. symbol
4. syllable
5. typical
6. mystery
7. myth
8. syrup
9. system
10. sympathy
11. symptom
12. hypnotize
13. lyrics
14. synonym
15. mythology

SKILL DRILL 4

Order of answers may vary in 1–3, 6–9, 12–14.

1. lyrics
2. symbol
3. system
4. crystal
5. hypnotize or mythology
6. mystery
7. mythology
8. sympathy
9. synonym
10. myth
11. syrup
12. pyramid
13. symptom
14. typical
15. syllable or sympathy

WORD GAME 8

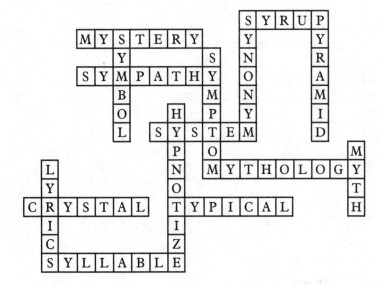

45

HOW WELL CAN YOU SPELL?

A. 1. syllable   2. system   3. sympathy   4. typical   5. pyramid
  6. symptom   7. myth

B. 8. syrup   9. mystery   10. mythology   11. symbol   12. hypnotize
  13. lyrics   14. synonym   15. crystal

An Additional Activity

Pass out pages from a magazine or a newspaper. Ask students to circle words that contain both long and short *i* sounds. Emphasize that students must be able to read the words they circle.

Supplementary Words

Lesson 8

gymnasium   mystify

gypsy   rhythm

hypnosis

---

9. Winging It
Pages 65–72

Objective

In Lesson 9 pupils are introduced to the *ph* combination that makes the sound of *f*. As in the past lessons, it is imperative that the teacher review the "Study List" words with the students for pronunciation purposes. It would also be wise to point out that most sounds in the English language are dependent upon the letters that follow and the *ph* sound is a good illustration of this principle. For example, the sound of *p* in *pen* is dependent upon the *e* just as the sound of *p* in *phase* is dependent upon the *h*. Emphasize that the *ph* combination always has the sound of the letter *f*. Both the "Skill Drill" exercises and the "Word Game" will give students the opportunity to become familiar with words containing this combination.

REVIEWING YOUR READING
  1. d   2. a   3. b   4. c   5. c   6. c   7. a   8. d

FIGURING THE FACTS
  1. T   2. F   3. T   4. T   5. F   6. T   7. F   8. T   9. T
  10. F

WHAT'S YOUR OPINION?
Answers will vary.

SKILL DRILL 1
  1. telegra(ph)   2. paragra(ph)   3. (ph)onics   4. autogra(ph)   5. (ph)otogra(ph)
  6. sym(ph)ony   7. em(ph)asize   8. tele(ph)one   9. (ph)ase   10. al(ph)abet
  11. biogra(ph)y   12. (ph)ysical   13. ele(ph)ant   14. trium(ph)   15. tro(ph)y

SKILL DRILL 2

1. symphony	2. physical	3. trophy	4. emphasize	5. biography
6. paragraph	7. autograph	8. elephant	9. telegraph	10. triumph
11. photograph	12. phase	13. telephone	14. alphabet	15. phonics

SKILL DRILL 3

1. alphabet	2. paragraph	3. autograph	4. phase	5. biography
6. photograph	7. emphasize	8. triumph	9. trophy	10. telegraph
11. telephone	12. physical	13. symphony	14. elephant	15. phonics

SKILL DRILL 4

Order of answers may vary in 2–6, 7–9.

1. emphasize	2. autograph	3. biography	4. paragraph	5. photograph
6. telegraph	7. phonics	8. symphony	9. telephone	10. trophy
11. elephant	12. alphabet	13. phase	14. physical	15. triumph

WORD GAME 9

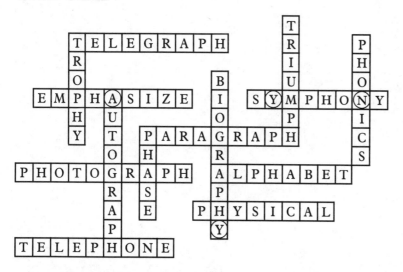

HOW WELL CAN YOU SPELL?

A.
1. emphasize	2. phonics	3. telegraph	4. paragraph	5. biography
6. phase	7. triumph			

B.
8. physical	9. alphabet	10. autograph	11. symphony	12. trophy
13. telephone	14. elephant	15. photograph		

An Additional Activity

Assign one ''Study List'' word to each student in the class. Ask each student to write the word once carefully and once incorrectly on two slips of paper or index cards. Allow students to test one another by holding up both spellings of the word while asking a fellow classmate to identify the correct spelling.

Lesson 9

chlorophyll	typhoid
graph	xylophone
photography	

---

10. Very Special Olympics

Pages 73–80

Objective

In this lesson students are exposed to the long *a* sound that is spelled *ai*. As in previous lessons, review of the "Study List" words will be helpful. It should also be mentioned to pupils that this particular grouping of letters is one variation on the spelling of the long *a* sound and cannot be considered a standard spelling for words containing the long *a* sound. *Ay* and *ae* are other alternative grapheme units that must also be thought of as letters that commonly work together in forming the sound of long *a*.

REVIEWING YOUR READING

1. b **2.** b **3.** b **4.** c **5.** d **6.** b **7.** c **8.** b

FIGURING THE FACTS

1. T **2.** T **3.** F **4.** T **5.** F **6.** F **7.** T **8.** T **9.** F **10.** F

WHAT'S YOUR OPINION?

Answers will vary.

SKILL DRILL 1

1. compl(ai)n **2.** p(ai)n **3.** d(ai)sy **4.** str(ai)n **5.** str(ai)ght
6. br(ai)d **7.** cl(ai)m **8.** expl(ai)n **9.** rem(ai)n **10.** f(ai)th
11. w(ai)ted **12.** fr(ai)l **13.** ch(ai)n **14.** av(ai)lable **15.** afr(ai)d

SKILL DRILL 2

1. daisy **2.** strain **3.** braid **4.** claim **5.** waited
6. explain **7.** available **8.** afraid **9.** straight **10.** chain
11. frail **12.** pain **13.** complain **14.** faith **15.** remain

SKILL DRILL 3

1. frail **2.** chain **3.** braid **4.** strain **5.** afraid
6. daisy **7.** explain **8.** straight **9.** available **10.** faith
11. remain **12.** pain **13.** waited **14.** claim **15.** complain

SKILL DRILL 4

Order of answers may vary in 2–7, 8–9.

1. claim
2. chain
3. complain
4. explain
5. pain
6. remain
7. strain
8. afraid
9. braid
10. available
11. faith
12. waited
13. straight
14. afraid or frail
15. daisy

WORD GAME 10

```
  S T R A I N
 E X P L A I N
W A I T E D
    C H A I N
  F A I T H
  B R A I D
A V A I L A B L E
```

```
    C O M P L A I N
F R A I L
D A I S Y
    R E M A I N
    P A I N
A F R A I D
    C L A I M
    S T R A I G H T
```

What is an event that shouldn't be missed? *SPECIAL OLYMPICS*

HOW WELL CAN YOU SPELL?

A.
1. strain
2. pain
3. braid
4. remain
5. claim
6. faith
7. complain

B.
8. daisy
9. straight
10. waited
11. chain
12. frail
13. afraid
14. available
15. explain

An Additional Activity

Give each student a page from an old telephone book. Ask them to look for names containing the *ai* combination and circle them. You may wish to have students read the names they find aloud.

Supplementary Words

Lesson 10

braid	drain	pain
brain	faint	plain
chair	grain	praise
daily	main	rain
dainty	maid	raise
dairy	nail	

Optional Testing List

---

11. The Great Stone Faces

Pages 81–88

Objective

Although all of the 15 words in the "Study List" begin with the letter combination *qu*, and the main objective of the lesson is to acquaint the students with this letter combination, there are other spelling patterns involved in the 15 words. The "Skill Drills" will draw the student's attention to many of them. However, this might be a good time for the teacher to review some patterns and rules of spelling previously learned. *Quarrel* and *quarry* contain double letters (refer to *Spell It Out*-Book 1, page 4.) *Quiet* applies to the *i before e* rule (refer to *Spell It Out*-Book 1, pages 124 and 132.) *Quit* applies to the doubling rule (refer to *Spell It Out*-Book 2, pages 4 and 28).

REVIEWING YOUR READING

1. b **2.** c **3.** a **4.** d **5.** d **6.** c **7.** b **8.** b

FIGURING THE FACTS

1. F **2.** T **3.** F **4.** T **5.** T **6.** F **7.** T **8.** T **9.** F
10. T

WHAT'S YOUR OPINION?

Answers will vary.

SKILL DRILL 1

1. (qu)it **2.** (qu)ickly **3.** (qu)arter **4.** (qu)alify **5.** (qu)iver
6. (qu)ilt **7.** (qu)arry **8.** (qu)estion **9.** (qu)otation **10.** (qu)artet
11. (qu)ota **12.** (qu)ite **13.** (qu)iet **14.** (qu)arrel **15.** (qu)antity

SKILL DRILL 2

1. question **2.** quickly **3.** quarry **4.** quarter **5.** quartet
6. quiver **7.** quotation **8.** quota **9.** qualify **10.** quit
11. quarrel **12.** quantity **13.** quilt **14.** quiet **15.** quite

SKILL DRILL 3

1. quarter **2.** quotation **3.** question **4.** qualify **5.** quite
6. quiet **7.** quarrel **8.** quarter **9.** quickly **10.** quit
11. quiver **12.** quilt **13.** quantity **14.** quarry **15.** quota

SKILL DRILL 4

Order of answers may vary in 1–4, 5–8, 9–10, 11–12.

1. quiet **2.** quilt **3.** quite **4.** quota **5.** qualify
6. quarrel **7.** quarter **8.** quartet **9.** question **10.** quotation
11. quarry **12.** quiver **13.** quantity **14.** quickly **15.** quit

WORD GAME 11

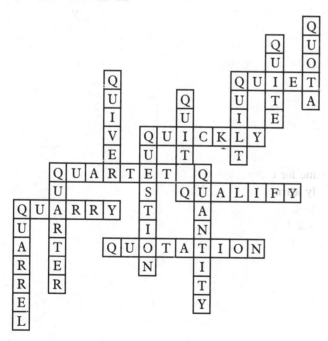

HOW WELL CAN YOU SPELL?

A. 1. quiver   2. quotation   3. quarter   4. quota   5. quite

     6. quiet   7. quantity

B. 8. quit   9. quarry   10. question   11. quarrel   12. quilt

     13. quartet   14. quickly   15. qualify

An Additional Activity

Mark several columns on the chalkboard and divide the class into teams. Ask one member of each team to go to the board and complete the spelling of a *qu* word. If the spelling is correct give that team a point. Continue to keep score as other students participate.

Supplementary Words

Lesson 11

quail	queen	quick	quote
quart	queer	quitter	

---

12. k. d. lang
Pages 89–96

Objective

In this lesson the *qu* combination is introduced as a letter cluster. Many different sounds are expressed by these letters and it is here that you have the opportunity to guide students in developing a strategy for figuring out the various sounds of this combination. For a general clue, you may wish to explain that in some instances the letter following the *qu* combination often provides the phonetic emphasis in pronunciation. For example, in the word *acquaint* we hear the long *a* sound after the *u* and in the word *squeeze* we hear the sound of the long *e*. This simple observation cannot be regarded as a panacea to the possible confusion that may develop as a student faces the many different pronunciations of the *qu* letter combination. It is one common pattern that may be noted amidst a host of unpredictable pronunciations.

REVIEWING YOUR READING

1. b   2. d   3. b   4. b   5. b   6. d   7. c   8. c

FIGURING THE FACTS

1. F; lower   2. F; Canada   3. T   4. T   5. F; Singer   6. F; youngest

7. F; pharmacist   8. T   9. T   10. T

WHAT'S YOUR OPINION?

Answers will vary.

SKILL DRILL 1

1. s(qu)irrel   2. s(qu)eeze   3. in(qu)ire   4. ac(qu)aint   5. s(qu)irt

6. s(qu)are   7. e(qu)al   8. s(qu)int   9. re(qu)ire   10. anti(qu)e

11. uni(qu)e   12. s(qu)awk   13. mos(qu)ito   14. a(qu)arium   15. ac(qu)ire

SKILL DRILL 2

1. squawk	2. square	3. aquarium	4. squirrel	5. squint
6. squeeze	7. mosquito	8. equal	9. require	10. inquire
11. antique	12. acquaint	13. squirt	14. unique	15. acquire

SKILL DRILL 3

1. acquaint	2. inquire	3. squeeze	4. squirrel	5. acquire
6. mosquito	7. squawk	8. antique	9. require	10. squint
11. aquarium	12. equal	13. square	14. squirt	15. unique

SKILL DRILL 4

Order of answers may vary in 1–2, 3–6, 7–8, 9–11.

1. antique	2. unique	3. square	4. squawk	5. squint
6. squirt	7. mosquito	8. squirrel	9. acquire	10. inquire
11. require	12. aquarium	13. squeeze	14. equal	15. acquaint

WORD GAME 12

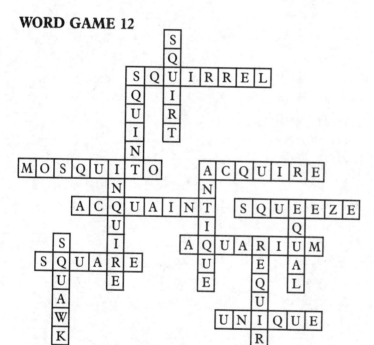

HOW WELL CAN YOU SPELL?

A.
1. acquaint	2. require	3. squint	4. squirrel	5. squirt
6. squawk	7. acquire			

B.
8. equal	9. mosquito	10. antique	11. unique	12. aquarium
13. squirrel	14. square	15. squeeze		

Supplementary Words

Lesson 12

Refer to the "Supplementary Words" for Lesson 11.

13. Peanut Power

Pages 97–104

Objective

This lesson and the next deal with *homophones*. Homophones, or words that sound alike but have different spellings and meanings, not only pose problems when misused but also when misspelled. It is most important that students understand the definitions of the words involved. The "Skill Drills" and "Word Game" give practice in this area, but it may also be wise for the teacher to assign extra drill work. It is also important for the teacher to point out the spelling problems in each particular word. For example, four of the words in the list apply to the *i before e* rule.

REVIEWING YOUR READING

1. b   2. b   3. a   4. d   5. b   6. d   7. c   8. c

FIGURING THE FACTS

1. T   2. T   3. F   4. F   5. T   6. T   7. T   8. T   9. F

10. T

WHAT'S YOUR OPINION?

Answers will vary.

SKILL DRILL 1

1. patience	2. patients	3. piece	4. peace	5. plain
6. plane	7. whole	8. hole	9. principle	10. principal
11. stationery	12. stationary	13. their	14. there	15. they're

SKILL DRILL 2

1. plain	2. plane	3. piece	4. peace	5. they're
6. these	7. their	8. patience	9. patients	10. hole
11. whole	12. stationary	13. stationery	14. principal	15. principle

SKILL DRILL 3

1. there	2. peace	3. plane	4. patience	5. their
6. piece	7. patients	8. plain	9. principal	10. stationery
11. principle	12. they're	13. whole	14. stationary	15. hole

SKILL DRILL 4

Order of answers may vary in 1-2, 4-5, 7-9, 10-12, 13-15.

1. plain	2. plane	3. patients	4. stationary	5. stationery
6. principal	7. their	8. there	9. they're	10. hole
11. whole	12. principle	13. patience	14. peace	15. piece

WORD GAME 13

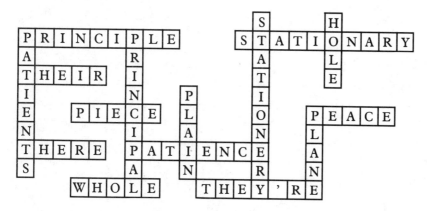

HOW WELL CAN YOU SPELL?

1. principle 2. patients 3. they're 4. patience 5. plane
6. stationary 7. their 8. stationary 9. plain 10. there
11. principal 12. piece 13. whole 14. peace 15. hole

An Additional Activity

Have students make up sentences using the homophones in this lesson.

Ask students to question each other on the correct usage and spelling of each homophone.

Supplementary Words

Lesson 13

aloud - allowed	male - mail	steel - steal
brake - break	sale - sail	week - weak
pair - pear	meat - meet	tide - tied
right - write	bee - be	die - dye
rap - wrap	flea - flee	no - know
pray - prey	see - sea	rode - road
wave - waive	seen - scene	lone - loan

---

14. Really Rolling

Pages 105–112

Objective

This lesson introduces 15 more homophones. As in the previous lesson, it is important that students not only know the spelling of each word, but also the definition.

REVIEWING YOUR READING

1. d   2. b   3. c   4. d   5. b   6. b   7. b   8. b

FIGURING THE FACTS
1. T **2.** F **3.** T **4.** F **5.** T **6.** F **7.** F **8.** T **9.** T

WHAT'S YOUR OPINION?
Answers will vary.

SKILL DRILL 1
1. wood	**2.** would	**3.** course	**4.** coarse	**5.** serial
6. cereal	**7.** herd	**8.** heard	**9.** rain	**10.** reign
11. through	**12.** threw	**13.** scent	**14.** sent	**15.** cent

SKILL DRILL 2
1. wood	**2.** herd	**3.** rain	**4.** cent	**5.** threw
6. scent	**7.** reign	**8.** heard	**9.** through	**10.** would
11. sent	**12.** course	**13.** cereal	**14.** serial	**15.** coarse

SKILL DRILL 3
1. cent	**2.** rain	**3.** herd	**4.** wood	**5.** cereal
6. heard	**7.** reign	**8.** scent	**9.** threw	**10.** serial
11. coarse	**12.** sent	**13.** would	**14.** through	**15.** course

SKILL DRILL 4
Order of answers may vary in 1–3, 4–5, 6–8.
1. course	**2.** through	**3.** would	**4.** cereal	**5.** heard
6. cent	**7.** scent	**8.** sent	**9.** wood	**10.** herd
11. reign	**12.** rain	**13.** threw	**14.** serial	**15.** coarse

WORD GAME 14

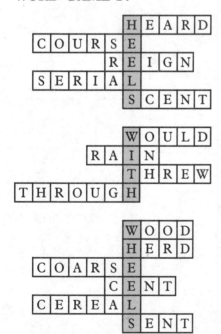

What is another name for roller skates? *HEELS WITH WHEELS*

HOW WELL CAN YOU SPELL?

1. would   2. through   3. coarse   4. serial   5. threw

6. rain   7. herd   8. wood   9. sent   10. cereal

11. heard   12. scent   13. course   14. reign   15. cent

Supplementary Words

Lesson 14

Refer to the "Supplementary Words" for Lesson 13.

---

15. Money

Pages 113–120

Objective

It is most appropriate that this lesson tells a short history of money, because the spelling words are all numbers. People most often use written numbers when writing checks or writing about money. Teachers should take this occasion to explain that some numbers like *eighty-eight* are like compound words, and that the hyphen joins the two words together to make them one. For an explanation of compound words, see *Spell It Out*-Book 1, pages 28 and 36.

REVIEWING YOUR READING

1. b   2. a   3. b   4. d   5. c   6. a   7. c   8. d

FIGURING THE FACTS

1. F   2. T   3. T   4. F   5. T   6. F   7. T   8. T   9. T

10. T

WHAT'S YOUR OPINION?

Answers will vary.

SKILL DRILL 1

1. fourteen   2. twenty-nine   3. ninety-two   4. seventy   5. eleven

6. twelve   7. forty   8. eighteen   9. four   10. eighty-eight

11. thirty-five   12. sixty-three   13. thirteen   14. fifty   15. fifteen

SKILL DRILL 2

1. twenty-nine   2. twelve   3. thirty-five   4. thirteen   5. sixty-three

6. seventy   7. ninety-two   8. fourteen   9. four   10. forty

11. fifty   12. fifteen   13. eleven   14. eighty-eight   15. eighteen

SKILL DRILL 3

1. Sixty three dollars and thirteen cents

2. Eighteen dollars

3. Thirty-five dollars and twelve cents

4. Forty dollars and twenty-nine cents
5. Eighty-eight dollars and eleven cents
6. Four dollars and fourteen cents
7. Ninety-two dollars and fifteen cents
8. Seventy dollars and fifteen cents
9. Twelve dollars and eighteen cents
10. Thirteen dollars
11. Sixty-three dollars and twenty-nine cents
12. Thirty-five dollars and forty cents
13. Seventy dollars and eighty-eight cents
14. Fourteen dollars and fifteen cents
15. Eleven dollars and fifty cents

SKILL DRILL 4

1. twelve
2. eighteen
3. thirteen
4. sixty-three
5. twenty-nine
6. seventy
7. eighty-eight
8. thirty-five
9. forty
10. fourteen
11. fifteen
12. eleven
13. fifty
14. four
15. ninety-two

WORD GAME 15

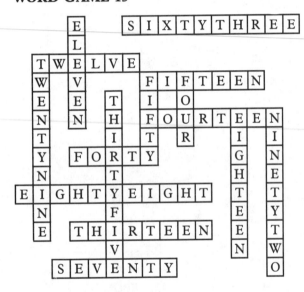

HOW WELL CAN YOU SPELL?

A.
1. eighteen
2. sixty-three
3. twenty-nine
4. thirty-five
5. forty
6. fifty
7. four
8. fourteen

B.
9. eleven
10. twelve
11. seventy
12. eighty-eight
13. fifteen
14. thirteen
15. ninety-two

Supplementary Words

Lesson 15

You may wish to add to the "Study List" of numbers.

Optional Testing List

Lessons 11–15

acquaint	patients	require
acquire	peace	scent
antique	piece	sent
aquarium	plain	seventy
cent	plane	sixty-three
cereal	principal	stationary
coarse	principle	stationery
course	qualify	square
eighteen	quantity	squawk
eighty-eight	quarter	squeeze
eleven	quartet	squint
equal	quarrel	squirrel
fifteen	quarry	squirt
fifty	question	their
forty	quickly	there
four	quiet	they're
fourteen	quilt	thirty-five
heard	quit	threw
herd	quite	through
hole	quiver	twelve
inquire	quota	twenty-nine
mosquito	quotation	unique
ninety-two	rain	wood
patience	reign	would

---

16. Protecting the Panda

Pages 121–128

Objective

This lesson is the first of five lessons that deals with the spelling rule for words ending in a silent *e*. The purpose of this particular lesson is to introduce the final silent *e* as a letter that appears at the end of many words in the English language, but for which no auditory clues are available. The teacher may wish to point out to students that a final silent *e* is often a clue to the pronunciation of a long vowel preceding it, as in the words *wake, made,* and *snake*. Remind pupils that when two vowels appear in a word the first one is usually pronounced like the name of its letter while the other is silent. When appearing as a final letter in a word the silent *e* serves as an indicator of how another letter should sound while forfeiting any sound of its own.

REVIEWING YOUR READING

1. c   **2.** b   **3.** d   **4.** d   **5.** b   **6.** c   **7.** d   **8.** a

FIGURING THE FACTS

1. F   2. T   3. F   4. F   5. F   6. F   7. F   8. F   9. T

10. T

WHAT'S YOUR OPINION?

Answers will vary.

SKILL DRILL 1

1. confus⨍	2. licens⨍	3. rejoic⨍	4. figur⨍	5. decreas⨍
6. arrang⨍	7. sacrific⨍	8. absolut⨍	9. resid⨍	10. absenc⨍
11. accus⨍	12. advertis⨍	13. creatur⨍	14. simpl⨍	15. introduc⨍

SKILL DRILL 2

1. advertise	2. creature	3. figure	4. license	5. confuse
6. rejoice	7. sacrifice	8. arrange	9. decrease	10. absence
11. absolute	12. reside	13. accuse	14. simple	15. introduce

SKILL DRILL 3

1. absence	2. advertise	3. arrange	4. creature	5. accuse
6. decrease	7. figure	8. sacrifice	9. simple	10. license
11. absolute	12. confuse	13. reside	14. rejoice	15. introduce

SKILL DRILL 4

Order of answers may vary in 2–3, 4–7, 10–14.

1. arrange	2. creature	3. figure	4. absence	5. introduce
6. rejoice	7. sacrifice	8. simple	9. absolute	10. accuse
11. advertise	12. confuse	13. decrease	14. license	15. reside

WORD GAME 16

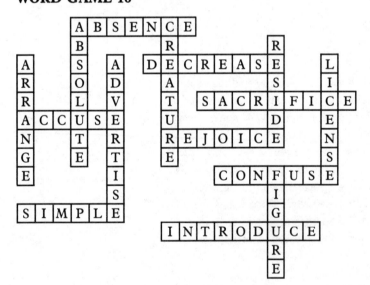

60

HOW WELL CAN YOU SPELL?

A. **1.** arrange **2.** creature **3.** figure **4.** advertise **5.** absolute

  6. rejoice **7.** introduce **8.** confuse

B. **9.** accuse **10.** simple **11.** reside **12.** sacrifice **13.** license

  14. absence **15.** decrease

An Additional Activity

Ask students to look through a particular study in their reading or language arts books and find as many words as possible ending in the silent *e*. You may wish to compile these words into a master list and pass it out to the entire class.

Supplementary Words

Lesson 16

ache	bite	complete	inside
alive	blade	confuse	issue
announce	blue	desire	pile
bare	bore	fire	raise
base	cane	grave	Senate

---

17. Steve Martin

Pages 129–136

Objective

The rule explained in this lesson says that when words end in a silent *e*, drop the *e* when adding a suffix that begins with a vowel. The teacher should take this opportunity to review vowels and suffixes. Since all of the words in the "Study List" end with the suffix *ing* or *able*, the suffixes may be interchanged. The "Study List" word *exciting* could also be *excitable*. The teacher should demonstrate this to the students, while emphasizing the fact that the rule still applies.

REVIEWING YOUR READING

1. d **2.** a **3.** a **4.** a **5.** b **6.** b **7.** d **8.** b

FIGURING THE FACTS

1. F **2.** T **3.** T **4.** T **5.** T **6.** T **7.** F **8.** T **9.** F
10. T

WHAT'S YOUR OPINION?

Answers will vary.

SKILL DRILL 1

1. us(able)
2. practic(ing)
3. excit(ing)
4. reduc(ing)
5. lov(able)
6. hop(ing)
7. shar(ing)
8. hav(ing)
9. mov(able)
10. mak(ing)
11. writ(ing)
12. becom(ing)
13. decid(ing)
14. serv(ing)
15. abus(ing)

SKILL DRILL 2

1. reducing
2. moving
3. exciting
4. having
5. serving
6. using
7. deciding
8. hoping
9. loving
10. writing
11. becoming
12. sharing
13. abusing
14. making
15. practicing

SKILL DRILL 3

1. excite
2. hoping
3. serve
4. becoming
5. lovable
6. usable
7. decide
8. sharing
9. make
10. move
11. abuse
12. writing
13. practice
14. reduce
15. having

SKILL DRILL 4

1. reducing
2. movable
3. serving
4. hoping
5. writing
6. sharing
7. abusing
8. making
9. practicing
10. becoming
11. deciding
12. lovable
13. usable
14. having
15. exciting

WORD GAME 17

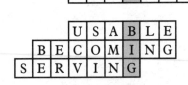

When Dr. Carleton P. Forbes stole the money, what did Steve Martin think it was? *A BIG CATASTROPHE*

HOW WELL CAN YOU SPELL?

A.
1. usable
2. becoming
3. serving
4. hoping
5. deciding
6. exciting
7. lovable

B.
8. practicing
9. having
10. Reducing
11. writing
12. sharing
13. moving
14. abusing
15. making

62

An Additional Activity

Use the list of words ending in silent *e* from Lesson 16 and ask students to apply the rule by adding appropriate suffixes.

Supplementary Words

Lesson 17

Refer to the "Supplementary Words" for Lesson 16.

---

18. The Heimlich Hug of Life

Pages 137–144

Objective

This lesson reviews the final silent *e* rule. Teachers should also explain to students that words like *breathe* drop the final silent *e* when adding a suffix that begins with a vowel. Therefore the "Study List" word *breathing* could also be made into *breathable*, according to the rule.

REVIEWING YOUR READING

1. a   **2.** d   **3.** a   **4.** a   **5.** d   **6.** c   **7.** d   **8.** b

FIRST THINGS FIRST

4   3   6   1   2   5

WHAT'S YOUR OPINION?

Answers will vary.

SKILL DRILL 1

1. celebrat(ing)	**2.** debat(able)	**3.** car(ing)	**4.** remov(able)	**5.** balanc(ing)
6. breath(ing)	**7.** sav(ing)	**8.** chok(ing)	**9.** freez(ing)	**10.** inflat(able)
11. ach(ing)	**12.** chas(ing)	**13.** din(ing)	**14.** trad(ing)	**15.** rescu(ing)

SKILL DRILL 2

1. choking	**2.** celebrating	**3.** aching	**4.** removing	**5.** caring
6. freezing	**7.** debating	**8.** rescuing	**9.** chasing	**10.** trading
11. saving	**12.** dining	**13.** breathing	**14.** balancing	**15.** inflating

SKILL DRILL 3

1. celebrating	**2.** caring	**3.** choking	**4.** removable	**5.** debatable
6. chasing	**7.** dining	**8.** breathing	**9.** balancing	**10.** inflatable
11. rescuing	**12.** trading	**13.** saving	**14.** freezing	**15.** aching

SKILL DRILL 4

1. rescue	**2.** saving	**3.** trade	**4.** breathe	**5.** dining
6. balancing	**7.** chase	**8.** removable	**9.** ache	**10.** caring
11. inflatable	**12.** debatable	**13.** freezing	**14.** celebrate	**15.** choking

WORD GAME 18

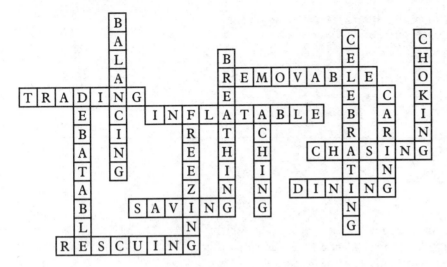

HOW WELL CAN YOU SPELL?

A. 1. breathing   2. trading   3. rescuing   4. freezing   5. choking

    6. inflatable   7. debatable

B. 8. saving   9. balancing   10. celebrating   11. chasing   12. dining

    13. removable   14. aching   15. caring

Supplementary Words

    Lesson 18

    Refer to the "Supplementary Words" for Lesson 16.

---

19. Colossus

Pages 145–152

Objective

    This lesson demonstrates what happens when adding a suffix that begins with a consonant to a word with a final silent e. It is primarily meant to reinforce what has already been learned in the previous three lessons. At this time, the teacher should make the students aware that the above rule does not apply when adding a suffix that begins with a consonant.

REVIEWING YOUR READING

1. c   2. d   3. b   4. b   5. c   6. b   7. b   8. c

FIGURING THE FACTS

1. T   2. F   3. F   4. T   5. T   6. T   7. F   8. T   9. F
10. T

WHAT'S YOUR OPINION?

Answers will vary.

SKILL DRILL 1

1. hope(ful)	2. safe(ly)	3. definite(ly)	4. sincere(ly)	5. entire(ly)
6. grace(ful)	7. absolute(ly)	8. nice(ly)	9. confine(ment)	10. scarce(ly)
11. pave(ment)	12. excite(ment)	13. care(ful)	14. bare(ly)	15. peace(ful)

SKILL DRILL 2

1. absolutely	2. entirely	3. excitement	4. barely	5. scarcely
6. peaceful	7. nicely	8. hopeful	9. graceful	10. pavement
11. safely	12. sincerely	13. confinement	14. careful	15. definitely

SKILL DRILL 3

1. entirely	2. scarcely	3. hopeful	4. excitement	5. sincerely
6. absolutely	7. barely	8. graceful	9. peaceful	10. nicely
11. safely	12. confinement	13. definitely	14. careful	15. pavement

SKILL DRILL 4

Order of answers may vary in 1–2, 3–5, 7–8, 9–10, 11–12.

1. graceful	2. peaceful	3. barely	4. nicely	5. safely
6. confinement	7. absolutely	8. definitely	9. careful	10. hopeful
11. entirely	12. scarcely	13. excitement	14. sincerely	15. pavement

WORD GAME 19

HOW WELL CAN YOU SPELL?

A. 1. careful   2. sincerely   3. barely   4. confinement   5. nicely

     6. safely   7. entirely

B. 8. scarcely   9. hopeful   10. absolutely   11. excitement   12. graceful

     13. peaceful   14. definitely   15. pavement

Supplementary Words

Lesson 19

Refer to the "Supplementary Words" for Lesson 16.

---

20. Tiger's Tale

Pages 153–160

Objective

This lesson is a review of the previous lesson and also a look at the special cases of words that end in *ce* or *ge*. The words included are the most common words that students will experience of this type, therefore memorization of the rule may not be necessary. However, teachers should stress the fact that all of the words retain the final silent *e* when adding *able* or *ous*. In order to strengthen the student's knowledge of the rule, the teacher should point out that we drop the final *e* when adding *ing*.

REVIEWING YOUR READING

1. c   2. a   3. c   4. c   5. c   6. a   7. a   8. d

FIGURING THE FACTS

1. T   2. T   3. F; people   4. T   5. F   6. T   7. T   8. T   9. T   10. F; no

WHAT'S YOUR OPINION?

Answers will vary.

SKILL DRILL 1

1. servi(ce)able   2. noti(ce)able   3. arran(ge)ment   4. coura(ge)ous   5. enga(ge)ment

6. advanta(ge)ous   7. mana(ge)able   8. tra(ce)able   9. announ(ce)ment   10. chan(ge)able

11. encoura(ge)ment   12. enti(ce)ment   13. exchan(ge)able   14. outra(ge)ous   15. pea(ce)able

SKILL DRILL 2

1. advantage   2. exchange   3. encouragement   4. peaceable   5. courageous

6. outrageous   7. manage   8. changeable   9. announce   10. noticeable

11. traceable   12. service   13. arrangement   14. entice   15. engagement

SKILL DRILL 3

1. traceable   2. serviceable   3. outrageous   4. peaceable   5. noticeable

6. manageable   7. changeable   8. enticement   9. engagement   10. encouragement

11. advantageous   12. arrangement   13. courageous   14. changeable   15. announcement

SKILL DRILL 4

Order of answers may vary in 1–5, 6–8, 9–15.

1. arrangement   2. enticement   3. engagement   4. encouragement   5. announcement
6. courageous   7. outrageous   8. advantageous   9. exchangeable   10. serviceable
11. changeable   12. traceable   13. manageable   14. noticeable   15. peaceable

WORD GAME 20

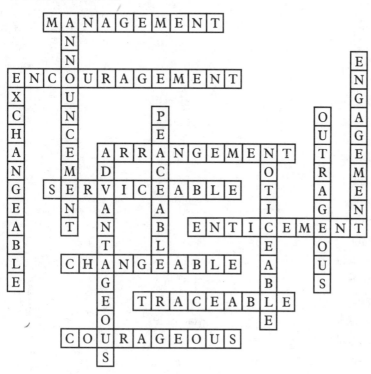

HOW WELL CAN YOU SPELL?

A.   1. noticeable   2. advantageous   3. announcement   4. traceable   5. outrageous
   6. management   7. engagement

B.   8. serviceable   9. peaceable   10. arrangement   11. encouragement   12. changeable
   13. enticement   14. exchangeable   15. courageous

Supplementary Words

Lesson 20

At this ability level few *ce, ge* words occur so an additional list of words has not been provided.

Optional Testing List

absence	debatable	nicely
absolute	deciding	noticeable
absolutely	decrease	outrageous
abusing	definitely	pavement
accuse	dining	peaceable
aching	encouragement	peaceful
advantageous	enticement	practicing
advertise	entirely	reducing
arrange	exchangeable	rejoice
arrangement	excitement	removable
balancing	exciting	rescuing
barely	figure	reside
becoming	freezing	sacrifice
breathing	graceful	safely
careful	having	saving
celebrating	hoping	serviceable
changeable	inflatable	serving
chasing	introduce	sharing
choking	license	simple
confinement	lovable	sincerely
confuse	making	traceable
courageous	manageable	trading
creature	movable	usable
		writing

Spell It Out—Book 3
Sample Lesson Plan

Here's Jay
Pages 1–8

Objectives
• To learn the rule: When a word ends in *y* preceded by a consonant, change the *y* to *i* before adding any suffix except *ing*.
• To improve the reading skills of finding the main idea, remembering details, and making inferences through experience and exercises

Motivation
For this lesson, you might begin with a discussion of Jay Leno's job on The Tonight Show. Ask whether anyone in the class has seen the show when Jay Leno is on it. If not, ask whether they have ever seen Jay Leno's routines anywhere else. Ask whether the students like his comedy routines.

Procedure
1. Ask questions about the opening picture. Who is in the picture? What is he doing? Why do you think the selection is entitled "Here's Jay"?

2. Have the students read the story silently. Instruct them to turn the page and complete the "Reviewing Your Reading" and "Figuring the Facts" exercises. Slower students should be encouraged to reread the selection before completing the "Figuring the Facts" exercise.

3. Choose students to go back and read the story aloud. Then ask individual students to read and answer the questions orally. This will provide a group activity and an answer check for all students.

4. Direct the students to answer the "What's Your Opinion?" exercise. This exercise may be used as a discussion activity, a writing activity, or both. Students may write their answers, then read them aloud. They may also discuss the differences in their answers. Since the student answers will vary, they will not appear in the *Guide and Answer Key* that follows.

5. Have students turn to the section entitled "Developing Spelling Skills." Explain that the words in dark type appear in the reading selection and that they demonstrate a particular pattern that applies to a spelling rule. The text will help you to explain the rule and its uses. Your demonstration should include a review of consonants and vowels. It would also be wise to review the meanings of the "Study List" words with the class and instruct students to refer to the

"Mini-Dictionary" (page 162) to find the definitions they are unsure of.

6. Direct the students to begin the series of "Skill Drills." The answers to the "Skill Drills" have been arranged in alphabetical order, where applicable, for your convenience. In "Skill Drill 4," for example, the students are asked to list the words from the "Study List" that end with the suffix *ing*. Although the students may list the words in any order, the Answer Key will list the words alphabetically.

7. After the "Skill Drills" and the "Word Game" have been completed and checked, direct the students to do "How Well Can You Spell?" a review quiz. You might want to have the students check their own work while you read the correct answers. This can be especially reinforcing because the students have the opportunity to correct their own errors and strengthen their own knowledge of the words.

Follow Up
1. Have the students do research in recent periodicals on Jay Leno or another comedian and prepare a short written report.

2. Ask students to make a list of words that end in *y* preceded by a consonant. Then have students exchange lists and add the suffixes *es*, *ed*, and *ing* to the words they have found. Explain that the three endings will not always be able to be added to all words.

3. The traditional spelling bee is a good reinforcement for a spelling lesson. The most common type is the two-team competition but some variations on the theme may increase student interest and participation. The following ideas can be adapted to small group or class activities where review of spelling words is the objective of the lesson.

Baseball—Organize a baseball spelling bee by dividing the class into two teams. Use the word list provided in the back of this teaching guide with four categories of difficulty. In the course of the game, the student may elect to try for a single (easy list), double (more difficult), triple (challenge), or home run (expert). If the word is spelled correctly the student can advance to the appropriate base. A run is scored when someone clears home plate, either through a home run or a run batted in. An incorrect spelling is out. Three outs and the other team is up at bat. The team with the most runs at the end of the bee wins.

Spell It Out—Book 3
Guide and Answer Key

1. Here's Jay
Pages 1–8

Objective
This lesson illustrates the rule for words that end in *y* preceded by a consonant. At this point it would be wise for the teacher to review vowels and consonants with the students. The ultimate aim of this and other lessons is to provide the student with a rule that is applicable to hundreds of other words, thus reducing his or her need to memorize and increasing the ability to transfer knowledge. The words for this and following chapters are chosen to provide the student with a model to follow. However, it is imperative that the teacher point out the similarities and differences in words. The ''Skill Drills'' and ''Word Game'' will reinforce this type of learning, but the teacher may wish to provide additional drill work.

REVIEWING YOUR READING
1. d   2. c   3. a   4. b   5. a   6. c   7. a   8. b

FIGURING THE FACTS
1. T   2. T   3. F   4. T   5. F   6. T   7. F   8. T   9. T
10. F

WHAT'S YOUR OPINION?
Answers will vary.

SKILL DRILL 1
1. injuries	2. multiplying	3. apologies	4. satisfied	5. classified
6. supplied	7. copied	8. magnifying	9. occupied	10. relying
11. authorities	12. studies	13. theories	14. defying	15. envying

SKILL DRILL 2
1. envying	2. authorities	3. injuries	4. relying	5. apologies
6. occupied	7. multiplying	8. defying	9. copied	10. magnifying
11. satisfied	12. theories	13. studies	14. classified	15. supplied

SKILL DRILL 3
1. satisfied	2. apologies	3. defying	4. classified	5. studies
6. theories	7. magnifying	8. copied	9. relying	10. injuries
11. authorites	12. Envying	13. supplies/ supplied	14. multiplying	15. occupied

SKILL DRILL 4

Order of answers may vary in 1–5, 6–10, 11–15.

1. defying	2. envying	3. magnifying	4. multiplying	5. relying
6. apologies	7. authorities	8. theories	9. injuries	10. studies
11. classified	12. copied	13. occupied	14. satisfied	15. supplied

WORD GAME 1

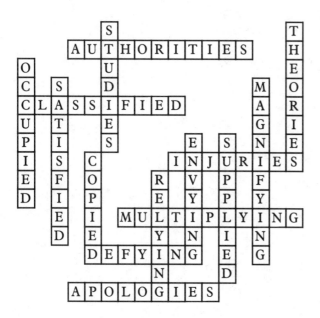

HOW WELL CAN YOU SPELL?

A.

1. satisfied	2. envying	3. magnifying	4. defying	5. apologies
6. supplied	7. authorities	8. injuries		

B.

9. relying	10. classified	11. theories	12. studies	13. copied
14. occupied	15. multiplying			

Additional Activities

Have students interchange the suffixes with the base words from the "Study List." Point out that words such as *classify* become *classified*, *classifying*, and *classifies*. Also have students compose their own sentences using another form of the word.

2. Up in Smoke

Pages 9–16

Objective

This chapter focuses on the second part of the rule dealing with words that end in *y*. That is, when a word ends in *y* preceded by a vowel the word is *not* changed when adding a suffix. The rule in this chapter is actually the exception to the rule in the previous chapter. The teacher should make the student aware of the relationship between these two "rules." Certainly, it would be easier for the student to remember the rules if their common points were demonstrated.

REVIEWING YOUR READING

1. c   **2.** d   **3.** a   **4.** b   **5.** b   **6.** c   **7.** a   **8.** b

FIGURING THE FACTS

Wording may vary for false answers.

1. F; more and more   **2.** F; white   **3.** T   **4.** F; less   **5.** T   **6.** F; high in the sky   **7.** F; five   **8.** T   **9.** F; often   **10.** F; tic-tac-toe

WHAT'S YOUR OPINION?

Answers will vary.

SKILL DRILL 1

1. displaying	**2.** journeys	**3.** surveying	**4.** swaying	**5.** annoyance
6. conveying	**7.** decoys	**8.** employer	**9.** relaying	**10.** strayed
11. alloys	**12.** betrayed	**13.** decayed	**14.** destroyed	**15.** disobeyed

SKILL DRILL 2

1. alloys	**2.** conveying	**3.** betrayed	**4.** swaying	**5.** strayed
6. disobeyed	**7.** relaying	**8.** journeys	**9.** employer	**10.** decayed
11. decoys	**12.** annoyance	**13.** displaying	**14.** destroyed	**15.** surveying

SKILL DRILL 3

1. surveying	**2.** disobeyed	**3.** strayed	**4.** swaying	**5.** conveying
6. betrayed	**7.** alloys	**8.** destroyed	**9.** displaying	**10.** annoyance
11. decoys	**12.** decayed	**13.** employer	**14.** journeys	**15.** relaying

SKILL DRILL 4

Order of answers may vary in 1–5, 7–9, 10–14.

1. surveying	**2.** displaying	**3.** swaying	**4.** relaying	**5.** conveying
6. employer	**7.** alloys	**8.** journeys	**9.** decoys	**10.** betrayed
11. disobeyed	**12.** decayed	**13.** strayed	**14.** destroyed	**15.** annoyance

WORD GAME 2

Where would you begin to look to find the skytypers? *UP*

HOW WELL CAN YOU SPELL?

A.
1. conveying 2. disobeyed 3. decayed 4. annoyance 5. journeys
6. decoys 7. alloys 8. surveying

B.
9. destroyed 10. displaying 11. swaying 12. betrayed 13. strayed
14. employer 15. relaying

---

3. Cliff Hanger

Pages 17–24

Objective

In this lesson the student is presented with a review of the basic rules of pluralization (adding *s* or *es* to the singular form). Also, the rule for pluralization of words that end in *ch* or *sh* (add *es*) is presented.

The teacher should review the formations of plurals in all types of words that have been covered thus far, specifically, words that end in *y*. It is imperative that the student catalog these rules and future rules in some way in order to have a mental reference for pluralization.

REVIEWING YOUR READING

1. b 2. a 3. b 4. d 5. b 6. c 7. a 8. a

FIGURING THE FACTS

Wording may vary for false answers.
1. F; El Capitan 2. T 3. T 4. F; one week 5. F; length of a climber's safety ropes 6. F; 27 pitches 7. T 8. F; bat tent 9. T 10. F; did not feel

WHAT'S YOUR OPINION?

Answers will vary.

SKILL DRILL 1

1. hatchets 2. sandwiches 3. sketches 4. inches 5. pouches
6. ambulances 7. characteristics 8. radishes 9. sheriffs 10. stitches
11. opinions 12. advantages 13. budgets 14. cheeses 15. crutches

SKILL DRILL 2

1. cheese 2. budget 3. ambulance 4. adventure 5. sheriff
6. crutch 7. sketch 8. stitch 9. sandwich 10. radish
11. pouch 12. opinion 13. inch 14. characteristic 15. hatchet

SKILL DRILL 3

1. cheeses 2. stitches 3. crutches 4. sandwiches 5. hatchets
6. radishes 7. pouches 8. opinions 9. budgets 10. ambulances
11. adventures 12. sheriffs 13. sketches 14. inches 15. characteristics

SKILL DRILL 4

Order of answers may vary in 1–2, 4–9.

1. budgets	**2.** hatchets	**3.** radishes	**4.** crutches	**5.** inches
6. pouches	**7.** sandwiches	**8.** sketches	**9.** stitches	**10.** cheeses
11. ambulances	**12.** opinions	**13.** adventures	**14.** sheriffs	**15.** characteristics

WORD GAME 3

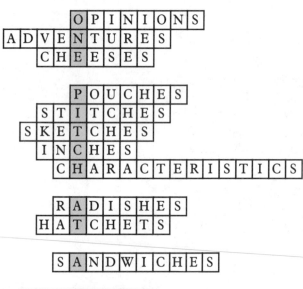

How did Beverly Johnson make it up El Capitan? *ONE PITCH AT A TIME*

HOW WELL CAN YOU SPELL?

A.
1. ambulances	**2.** sheriffs	**3.** characteristics	**4.** pouches	**5.** crutches
6. stitches	**7.** adventures	**8.** budgets		

B.
9. opinions	**10.** sandwiches	**11.** inches	**12.** radishes	**13.** cheeses
14. sketches	**15.** hatchets			

Additional Activities

Have students return to Lessons 1 and 2 and select nouns from the reading selections. Instruct the students to pluralize those words and present them to the class, citing the rule used.

Supplementary Words

accessory	brush	dish
allowance	bush	flash
appliance	church	latch
batch	clash	match
beach	crunch	

---

4. The Moose Is Loose!
Pages 25–32

Objective
This lesson introduces one more rule for pluralization, and reviews the previously learned rules for pluralization. The new rule states that words ending in *x* form their plural by adding es to the singular.

REVIEWING YOUR READING
1. b   **2.** d   **3.** c   **4.** b   **5.** a   **6.** a   **7.** b   **8.** b

FIGURING THE FACTS
Wording may vary for false answers.
1. T   **2.** F; a deep a-e-i-o-u   **3.** T   **4.** T   **5.** F; attract females   **6.** T
7. F; different from   **8.** T   **9.** F; Male   **10.** T

WHAT'S YOUR OPINION?
Answers will vary.

SKILL DRILL 1
1. parades	**2.** schedules	**3.** trophies	**4.** activities	**5.** bushes
6. foxes	**7.** magazines	**8.** reflexes	**9.** speeches	**10.** valleys
11. ambulances	**12.** classes	**13.** hatches	**14.** matches	**15.** wishes

SKILL DRILL 2
1. speech	**2.** schedule	**3.** reflex	**4.** parade	**5.** fox
6. class	**7.** bush	**8.** ambulance	**9.** activity	**10.** match
11. magazine	**12.** hatchet	**13.** wish	**14.** valley	**15.** trophy

SKILL DRILL 3
1. trophies	**2.** speeches	**3.** schedules	**4.** magazines	**5.** hatches
6. reflexes	**7.** parades	**8.** foxes	**9.** activities	**10.** matches
11. classes	**12.** bushes	**13.** ambulances	**14.** wishes	**15.** valleys

SKILL DRILL 4
Order of answers may vary in 1–2, 3–4, 5–6, 7–8, 9–10, 11–12, 13–14.
1. foxes	**2.** reflexes	**3.** matches	**4.** speeches	**5.** bushes
6. wishes	**7.** classes	**8.** ambulances	**9.** valleys	**10.** schedules
11. magazines	**12.** parades	**13.** activities	**14.** trophies	**15.** hatchets

WORD GAME 4

HOW WELL CAN YOU SPELL?

A. 1. wishes   2. hatchets   3. foxes   4. reflex   5. ambulances
    6. valleys   7. schedules   8. speeches

B. 9. activities   10. trophies   11. parades   12. magazines   13. bushes
    14. matches   15. classes

---

5. Cowkids

Pages 33–40

Objective

This lesson introduces another rule for pluralization. Nouns that end in
o preceded by a vowel add *s* to form the plural. If the noun ends in *o*
preceded by a consonant add *es* to form the plural. The exceptions are musical
terms and instruments that end in *o*. All form the plural by adding *s*. Since
this is a three-part rule, it is imperative that the teacher guide students
through the explanation and help them to coordinate their knowledge of the
rule.

REVIEWING YOUR READING

1. b   2. d   3. a   4. d   5. a   6. c   7. b   8. c

FIGURING THE FACTS

Wording may vary for false answers.

1. T   2. F; largest   3. T   4. F; wildest is goat tying   5. F; a thousand   6. F;
three legs   7. T   8. T   9. T   10. F; eight seconds

WHAT'S YOUR OPINION?

Answers will vary.

SKILL DRILL 1

1. rodeos	2. potatoes	3. pianos	4. stereos	5. buffaloes
6. volcanoes	7. tomatoes	8. radios	9. portfolios	10. studios
11. heroes	12. banjos	13. tornadoes	14. sopranos	15. shampoos

SKILL DRILL 2

1. shampoo	2. rodeo	3. buffalo	4. radio	5. potato
6. portfolio	7. tomato	8. tornado	9. piano	10. studio
11. hero	12. stereo	13. soprano	14. banjo	15. volcano

SKILL DRILL 3

1. radios	2. tornadoes	3. tomatoes	4. portfolios	5. potatoes
6. buffaloes	7. rodeos	8. stereos	9. heroes	10. volcanoes
11. sopranos	12. studios	13. pianos	14. shampoos	15. banjos

SKILL DRILL 4

Order of answers may vary in 1–3, 4–9, 10–15.

1. banjo, banjos	2. piano, pianos	3. soprano, sopranos	4. buffalo, buffaloes	5. hero, heroes
6. potato, potatoes	7. tomato, tomatoes	8. tornado, tornadoes	9. volcano, volcanoes	10. portfolio, portfolios
11. radio, radios	12. rodeo, rodeos	13. shampoo, shampoos	14. stereo, stereos	15. studio, studios

WORD GAME 5

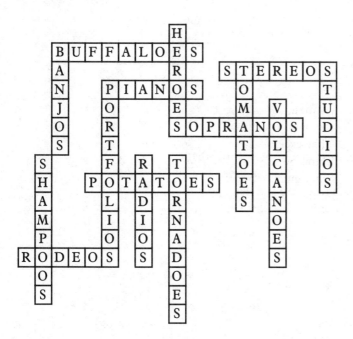

77

HOW WELL CAN YOU SPELL?

A.   **1.** pianos   **2.** shampoos   **3.** stereos   **4.** portfolios   **5.** radios

     6. sopranos   **7.** volcanoes   **8.** buffaloes

B.   **9.** studios   **10.** potatoes   **11.** banjos   **12.** heroes   **13.** rodeos

     14. tomatoes   **15.** tornadoes

An Additional Activity

To reinforce these rules write words from Lessons 3, 4, and 5 on slips of paper. Divide the class into teams. Ask each student to take a word. Give students time to read the word, decide which rule applies and why. Then let students explain their answer to their classmates. Record points for each correct answer. The team with the most points wins.

Optional Testing List

Lessons 1-5

activities	displaying	multiplying
adventures	decayed	occupied
alloys	decoys	opinions
ambulances	defying	pouches
annoyance	destroyed	radishes
apologies	disobeyed	relaying
authorities	employer	relying
betrayed	envying	sandwiches
budgets	finally	satisfied
characteristics	hatchets	sheriffs
cheeses	inches	sketches
conveying	initially	stitches
copied	injuries	strayed
classified	journeys	studies
crutches	magnifying	supplied

6. Greenpeace

Pages 41–48

Objective

This lesson introduces the final rule for pluralization. Some words that end in *f* or *fe* form their plurals by dropping the *f* or *fe* and adding *ves*. The "Study List" contains most of the words that a student will use that apply to this rule. It is important that the teacher stresses the fact that these are irregular plurals and must be memorized.

REVIEWING YOUR READING

1. c   **2.** b   **3.** d   **4.** c   **5.** a   **6.** b   **7.** c   **8.** c

FIGURING THE FACTS

Wording may vary for false answers.

1. T **2.** F; whales **3.** T **4.** F; protect mother whales and their calves **5.** F; harpoon **6.** T **7.** T **8.** F; 1960s **9.** F; Canadians and Americans **10.** T

WHAT'S YOUR OPINION?

Answers will vary.

SKILL DRILL 1

1. thieves	**2.** ourselves	**3.** loaves	**4.** elves	**5.** lives
6. wolves	**7.** halves	**8.** shelves	**9.** leaves	**10.** calves
11. yourselves	**12.** hooves	**13.** knives	**14.** wives	**15.** wharves

SKILL DRILL 2

1. loaf	**2.** wolf	**3.** thief	**4.** shelf	**5.** knife
6. half	**7.** wife	**8.** wharf	**9.** ourself	**10.** leaf
11. elf	**12.** yourself	**13.** life	**14.** hoof	**15.** calf

SKILL DRILL 3

1. yourselves	**2.** hooves	**3.** halves	**4.** wolves	**5.** shelves
6. knives	**7.** wharves	**8.** ourselves	**9.** leaves	**10.** elves
11. lives	**12.** calves	**13.** loaves	**14.** thieves	**15.** wives

SKILL DRILL 4

Order of answers may vary in 3–5, 9–11, 13–14.

1. thief, thieves	**2.** leaf, leaves	**3.** elf, elves	**4.** ourself, ourselves	**5.** shelf, shelves
6. yourself, yourselves	**7.** loaf, loaves	**8.** hoof, hooves	**9.** knife, knives	**10.** life, lives
11. wife, wives	**12.** wharf, wharves	**13.** calf, calves	**14.** half, halves	**15.** wolf, wolves

WORD GAME 6

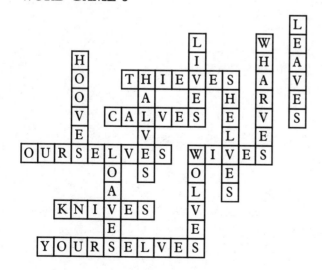

79

HOW WELL CAN YOU SPELL?

A.
1. knives
2. lives
3. wives
4. hooves
5. wolves
6. ourselves
7. shelves
8. thieves

B.
9. halves
10. loaves
11. wharves
12. elves
13. yourselves
14. calves
15. leaves

Additional Activities

Have students make a comprehensive list of "Study List" words from the last five lessons. Then have them change all the words to plurals. Ask students to compose sentences to strengthen their knowledge on the usage of plurals.

7. Riches From the Deep

Pages 49–56

Objective

The object of this lesson is to discuss the rule for changing adjectives to adverbs. Simply add the suffix *ly* to change most adjectives to adverbs.

Learning the rule is of little value if the student does not know what adjectives and adverbs are. The text gives a simple explanation. The teacher should explain the concepts further.

The lesson also provides a review of the rule for adding a suffix to words that ends in *y*. The teacher should draw attention to the words in the "Study List" that apply to this rule.

REVIEWING YOUR READING

1. b   2. c   3. d   4. a   5. b   6. a   7. a   8. b

FIGURING THE FACTS

Wording may vary for false answers.

1. F; Spanish sailing vessels   2. T   3. F; hit a coral reef   4. F; Maine   5. F; 44 years   6. F; governor   7. F; Massachusetts Bay Colony   8. T   9. F; *Concepcion*
10. T

WHAT'S YOUR OPINION?

Answers will vary.

SKILL DRILL 1

1. cleverly	2. entirely	3. accurately	4. clumsily	5. wearily
6. certainly	7. nearly	8. recently	9. immediately	10. coarsely
11. desperately	12. absolutely	13. luckily	14. separately	15. rapidly

SKILL DRILL 2

1. absolutely	2. entirely	3. immediately	4. wearily	5. separately
6. luckily	7. nearly	8. rapidly	9. recently	10. clumsily
11. accurately	12. cleverly	13. certainly	14. coarsely	15. desperately

SKILL DRILL 3

1. desperately	2. immediately	3. luckily	4. nearly	5. rapidly
6. recently	7. separately	8. wearily	9. absolutely	10. coarsely
11. certainly	12. cleverly	13. accurately	14. entirely	15. clumsily

SKILL DRILL 4

Order of answers may vary in 1–4, 6–7, 9–10, 11–12, 13–14.

1. accurately	2. desperately	3. immediately	4. separately	5. coarsely
6. nearly	7. wearily	8. absolutely	9. clumsily	10. luckily
11. rapidly	12. certainly	13. recently	14. entirely	15. cleverly

WORD GAME 7

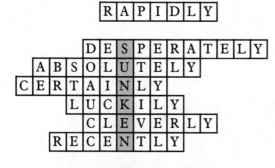

What do you call riches from the deep? *A SUNKEN TREASURE*

HOW WELL CAN YOU SPELL?

A.
1. certainly
2. rapidly
3. luckily
4. coarsely
5. separately
6. accurately
7. immediately
8. desperately

B
9. recently
10. clumsily
11. absolutely
12. cleverly
13. entirely
14. nearly
15. wearily

An Additional Activity

Have students compose sentences using the words from the "Study List" first as adjectives and then as adverbs.

Supplementary Words

attractive	curious
bare	decent
cheap	extreme
complete	haphazard
convenient	intense
courageous	perfect
courteous	serious

---

8. Pearlie Mae

Pages 57–64

Objective

This lesson reviews the rule from the previous chapter by discussing the rule for changing adjectives that end in *l* to adverbs. To change adjectives that end in *l* to adverbs, add the suffix *ly*. At this time the teacher may refer to Spell It Out-Book 1, page 76 for a discussion of words that end in *ful*.

REVIEWING YOUR READING

1. c   2. a   3. d   4. b   5. d   6. a   7. c   8. b

FIGURING THE FACTS

1. T   2. T   3. F   4. T   5. T   6. F   7. T   8. T   9. F
10. F

WHAT'S YOUR OPINION?

Answers will vary.

SKILL DRILL 1

1. respectfully
2. accidentally
3. occasionally
4. really
5. cheerfully
6. finally
7. initially
8. totally
9. naturally
10. practically
11. actually
12. faithfully
13. gracefully
14. legally
15. locally

SKILL DRILL 2

1. practically
2. really
3. actually
4. cheerfully
5. faithfully
6. finally
7. initially
8. gracefully
9. legally
10. respectfully
11. totally
12. accidentally
13. naturally
14. occasionally
15. locally

SKILL DRILL 3

Order of answers may vary in 4–5, 6-9, 12-13, 14–15.

1. totally
2. occasionally
3. accidentally
4. actually
5. practically
6. cheerfully
7. gracefully
8. faithfully
9. respectfully
10. legally
11. really
12. naturally
13. finally
14. locally
15. initially

SKILL DRILL 4

1. locally
2. occasionally
3. naturally
4. accidentally
5. totally
6. respectfully
7. legally
8. gracefully
9. finally
10. faithfully
11. cheerfully
12. really
13. initially
14. practically
15. actually

WORD GAME 8

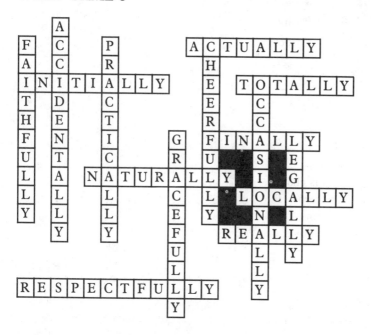

HOW WELL CAN YOU SPELL?

A.
1. faithfully
2. locally
3. totally
4. initially
5. legally
6. naturally
7. respectfully

B.
8. actually
9. occasionally
10. accidentally
11. practically
12. finally
13. really
14. gracefully
15. cheerfully

An Additional Activity

Have students clip an article out of a newspaper. Ask them to list all the adjectives they can find. Change the adjectives they find to adverbs. Then have them look for adverbs and change them to adjectives.

Supplementary Words

awfully	manually
carefully	peacefully
ideally	thoughtfully
incidentally	uneventfully
logically	ungratefully
	wonderfully

---

9. The Dinner Party

Pages 65–72

Objective

This lesson introduces two rules for the use of the *apostrophe*. (1) The apostrophe is used to show possession. (b) The apostrophe is used to show that a letter is missing in a contraction.

The teacher should use this opportunity to discuss the possessive case. The text gives a simplified explanation. However, it would be wise for the teacher to provide additional clarification and drill work.

REVIEWING YOUR READING

1. c   2. b   3. c   4. b   5. a   6. c   7. b   8. a

FIGURING THE FACTS

Wording may vary for false answers.

1. F; five   2. F; sculpture, painting, and needlework   3. T   4. T   5. T   6. T
7. F; linen   8. T   9. T   10. F; triangles

WHAT'S YOUR OPINION?

Answers will vary.

SKILL DRILL 1

1. shouldn't   2. secretary or secretarys'   3. it's   4. passenger's or passengers'   5. wouldn't
6. women's   7. where's   8. couldn't   9. doesn't   10. mechanic's or mechanics'
11. artist's or artists'   12. won't   13. haven't   14. we'll   15. you've

SKILL DRILL 2

1. mechanic's   2. passenger's   3. couldn't   4. haven't   5. artist's
6. won't   7. women's   8. shouldn't   9. secretary's   10. doesn't
11. it's   12. wouldn't   13. where's   14. we'll   15. you've

SKILL DRILL 3

1. The artist's studio contains many beautiful paintings.

2. The mechanic's tools are in the bag.

3. Tom couldn't attend the class picnic.

4. The passenger's luggage is on the train.

5. I haven't been to the library for two days.

6. Sandra won't be taking the bus today.

7. The women's paintings will be on display tonight.

8. A person shouldn't go swimming after eating a big meal.

9. The secretary's desk is in the corner.

10. The whole trip doesn't take more than three hours.

11. It's ten minutes past four o'clock.

12. You've stored plenty of food in the refrigerator.

13. I wouldn't do that if I were you.

14. Where's the vacuum cleaner?

15. We're going away, but we'll be right back.

SKILL DRILL 4

Order of answers may vary in 1–5, 6–7, 9–14.

1. artist's	2. mechanic's	3. passenger's	4. secretary's	5. women's
6. it's	7. where's	8. we'll	9. couldn't	10. doesn't
11. haven't	12. shouldn't	13. won't	14. wouldn't	15. you've

WORD GAME 9

What was missing at the "Dinner Party"? *FOOD*

HOW WELL CAN YOU SPELL?

A.
1. couldn't	2. doesn't	3. we'll	4. shouldn't	5. haven't
6. you've	7. it's			

B.
8. mechanic's	9. won't	10. where's	11. women's	12. secretary's
13. artist's	14. passenger's	15. wouldn't		

---

10. True Colors

Pages 73–80

Objective

This lesson introduces the first of two lessons on *vowel combinations*. The focus is on words that have vowels that are not ordinarily heard in common pronunciation. Many of the combinations that are exemplified in the lesson are used again and again in the English language. The student's skill in recognizing these combinations will increase his or her knowledge of words containing similar combinations.

REVIEWING YOUR READING

1. c 2. d 3. b 4. c 5. a 6. a 7. b 8. c

FIGURING THE FACTS

Wording may vary for false answers.

1. T 2. F; grade 3. T 4. F; do 5. F; only half of 6. T 7. T
8. T 9. T 10. F; blue

WHAT'S YOUR OPINION?

Answers will vary.

SKILL DRILL 1

1. bouquet	**2.** optional	**3.** recruit	**4.** theater	**5.** associate
6. avoid	**7.** committee	**8.** career	**9.** pursuit	**10.** superior
11. understood	**12.** autobiography	**13.** biscuit	**14.** essential	**15.** guessing

SKILL DRILL 2

1. guessing	**2.** bouquet	**3.** theater	**4.** essential	**5.** understood
6. associate	**7.** autobiography	**8.** avoid	**9.** career	**10.** optional
11. pursuit	**12.** recruit	**13.** superior	**14.** committee	**15.** biscuit

SKILL DRILL 3

1. understood	**2.** associate	**3.** career	**4.** optional	**5.** pursuit
6. essential	**7.** autobiography	**8.** avoid	**9.** guessing	**10.** bouquet
11. theater	**12.** recruit	**13.** superior	**14.** committee	**15.** biscuit

SKILL DRILL 4

Order of answers may vary in 1–2, 4–6, 8–9, 11–13, 14–15.

1. career	**2.** committee	**3.** understood	**4.** optional	**5.** superior
6. autobiography	**7.** avoid	**8.** essential	**9.** associate	**10.** theater
11. biscuit	**12.** recruit	**13.** pursuit	**14.** guessing	**15.** bouquet

WORD GAME 10

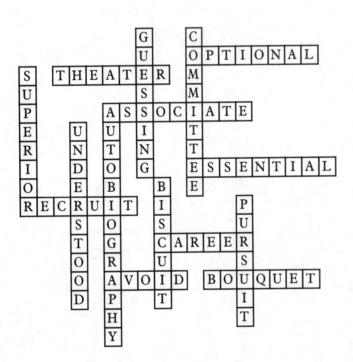

HOW WELL CAN YOU SPELL?

A. 1. understood 2. avoid 3. committee 4. career 5. superior
6. autobiography 7. optional

B 8. theater 9. recruit 10. biscuit 11. essential 12. associate
13. Guessing 14. bouquet 15. pursuit

An Additional Activity

Have students review the "Study Lists" in all the lessons that they have completed. Ask students to list all the words that contain vowel combinations. Have students compare lists to check their answers.

Supplementary Words

influence	obedient
influenza	ointment
January	option
language	overhaul
leather	patience
leisure	premium
maintenance	rebuild
maroon	region

Optional Testing List

Lessons 6–10.

activities	lives
artist's	loaves
associate	optional
autobiography	ourselves
avoid	passenger's
biscuit	pianos
bouquet	portfolios
buffaloes	potatoes
calves	pursuit
career	radios
committee	recruit
couldn't	rodeos
doesn't	secretary's
elves	shampoo
essential	shelves
guessing	shouldn't
halves	speeches
haven't	stereos
heroes	studios
hooves	superior
it's	theater
knives	thieves
leaves	tomatoes

tornadoes	wives
trophies	wolves
understood	won't
volcanoes	wouldn't
we'll	women's
wharves	yourselves
where's	you've

11. Ships of the Desert

Pages 81–88

Objective

Like the previous lesson, this lesson deals with words containing vowel combinations. Words with obvious vowel sounds like the *ua* in *individual* have purposely been intermingled with those that have no auditory clues like *lieutenant* to train the student to be wary of unusual vowel sounds. As in all learning of this type, visual recognition of the word is imperative. The "Skill Drills" and "Word Game" will especially reinforce this learning.

REVIEWING YOUR READING

1. b   2. a   3. a   4. b   5. c   6. a   7. a   8. d

FIGURING THE FACTS

Wording may vary for false answers.

1. T   2. F; half a ton   3. T   4. F; are a means   5. F; will drink more   6. F; twice   7. F; won't   8. F; are not always eager   9. T   10. T

WHAT'S YOUR OPINION?

Answers will vary.

SKILL DRILL 1

1. ser(iou)s   2. val(ua)ble   3. r(ea)lize   4. nerv(ou)s   5. ambit(iou)s
6. c(oo)perate   7. c(ou)nterf(ei)t   8. vac(uu)m   9. rel(ia)ble   10. procl(ai)m
11. man(ua)l   12. appr(oa)ch   13. c(au)t(io)n   14. individ(ua)l   15. l(ieu)tenant

SKILL DRILL 2

1. vacuum   2. ambitious   3. approach   4. caution   5. proclaim
6. realize   7. reliable   8. serious   9. lieutenant   10. manual
11. nervous   12. cooperate   13. counterfeit   14. individual   15. valuable

SKILL DRILL 3

1. manual   2. valuable   3. individual   4. ambitious   5. serious
6. caution   7. cooperate   8. vacuum   9. realize   10. proclaim
11. reliable   12. lieutenant   13. approach   14. counterfeit   15. nervous

SKILL DRILL 4

Order may vary in 1–3, 8–11.

1. individual
2. manual
3. valuable
4. proclaim
5. reliable
6. lieutenant
7. approach
8. ambitious
9. counterfeit
10. nervous
11. serious
12. caution
13. cooperate
14. vacuum
15. realize

WORD GAME 11

What do camels have that other animals do not? *HUMPS*

HOW WELL CAN YOU SPELL?

A.
1. proclaim
2. realize
3. vacuum
4. approach
5. manual
6. ambitious
7. lieutenant
8 caution

B.
9. valuable
10. nervous
11. counterfeit
12. reliable
13. cooperate
14. individual
15. serious

An Additional Activity

Assign each student two or three pages of a dictionary. Have each student make a list of words he or she finds that contain vowel combinations. Each student should present his or her findings to the class.

Supplementary Words

acclaim	coarse	detail
account	compound	disease
ahead	continental	encounter
casual	courtesy	hoarse
chauffeur	daughter	impair

---

12. Free Wheeling

Pages 89–96

Objective

This lesson presents three commonly confused endings: *ise*, *ice*, and *ize*. The "Study List" words have been chosen to emphasize the differences in these endings. Again, memorization and application are of prime importance.

Too often in our language these endings are not properly pronounced. The result is often a misspelling of words with these endings. The teacher should emphasize the pronunciation as well as the spelling and the meaning of each word.

REVIEWING YOUR READING

1. d
2. b
3. c
4. c
5. c
6. d
7. a
8. c

FIGURING THE FACTS

Wording may vary for false answers.

1. T
2. F; human power
3. F; 1690
4. T
5. T
6. T
7. T
8. T
9. F; human-driven
10. F; two years

WHAT'S YOUR OPINION?

Answers will vary.

SKILL DRILL 1

1. prejud(ice)	**2.** patron(ize)	**3.** standard(ize)	**4.** disgu(ise)	**5.** improv(ise)
6. apprent(ice)	**7.** summar(ize)	**8.** pract(ice)	**9.** item(ize)	**10.** accompl(ice)
11. critic(ize)	**12.** exerc(ise)	**13.** advert(ise)	**14.** spl(ice)	**15.** rev(ise)

SKILL DRILL 2

1. improvise	**2.** exercise	**3.** apprentice	**4.** advertise	**5.** summarize
6. splice	**7.** revise	**8.** prejudice	**9.** practice	**10.** patronize
11. itemize	**12.** standardize	**13.** accomplice	**14.** disguise	**15.** criticize

SKILL DRILL 3

1. itemize	**2.** accomplice	**3.** improvise	**4.** apprentice	**5.** patronize
6. criticize	**7.** summarize	**8.** standardize	**9.** prejudice	**10.** exercise
11. advertise	**12.** disguise	**13.** practice	**14.** splice	**15.** revise

SKILL DRILL 4

Order of answers may vary in 1–5, 6–10, 11–15.

1. accomplice	**2.** apprentice	**3.** practice	**4.** prejudice	**5.** splice
6. advertise	**7.** disguise	**8.** exercise	**9.** improvise	**10.** revise
11. criticize	**12.** itemize	**13.** patronize	**14.** standardize	**15.** summarize

WORD GAME 12

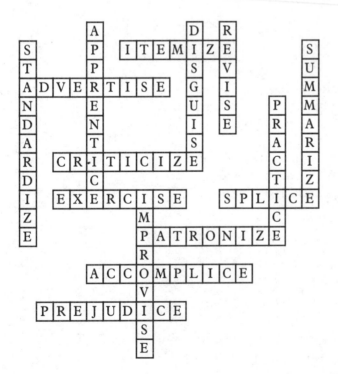

HOW WELL CAN YOU SPELL?

A.
1. disguise
2. accomplice
3. splice
4. summarize
5. criticize
6. exercise
7. revise
8. apprentice

B.
9. advertise
10. practice
11. itemize
12. patronize
13. improvise
14. prejudice
15. standardize

An Additional Activity

Divide students into three groups, each representing one of the three endings: *ise, ice,* and *ize.* Challenge each group to find as many words for their group as they can (scanning other school books such as history or science books). The group with the most words wins. You may wish to compile the words found into a master list and hand it out to the class.

Supplementary Words

advise	penalize
device	precipice
merchandise	precise
naturalize	realize
novice	recognize
otherwise	seize
paradise	utilize
pasteurize	

---

13. Her Best Shot

Pages 97–104

Objective

In this lesson students are exposed to the ways that the *i* sound is spelled. Also, the lesson covers the spelling of the *ct* consonant combination. The lesson is basically a look at some commonly confused consonant sounds.

Pronunciation plays a major role in the learning of these spellings. It is important that the teacher make sure students are clear on the pronunciation of the "Study List" words.

REVIEWING YOUR READING

1. b
2. d
3. c
4. c
5. a
6. c
7. a
8. b

FIGURING THE FACTS

Wording may vary for false answers.
1. T
2. F; father
3. T
4. T
5. F; strength and balance
6. T
7. F; less
8. F; a quarter
9. F; rock
10. F; 20

WHAT'S YOUR OPINION?

Answers will vary.

SKILL DRILL 1

1. ve⟨ge⟩table	**2.** privile⟨ge⟩	**3.** inspe⟨ct⟩or	**4.** milea⟨ge⟩	**5.** langua⟨ge⟩
6. wrecka⟨ge⟩	**7.** constru⟨ct⟩	**8.** salva⟨ge⟩	**9.** spe⟨ct⟩ators	**10.** impa⟨ct⟩
11. mana⟨ge⟩d	**12.** knowle⟨dg⟩e	**13.** distra⟨ct⟩	**14.** compa⟨ct⟩	**15.** attra⟨ct⟩

SKILL DRILL 2

1. language	**2.** managed	**3.** mileage	**4.** wreckage	**5.** privilege
6. inspector	**7.** spectators	**8.** salvage	**9.** vegetable	**10.** attract
11. knowledge	**12.** compact	**13.** construct	**14.** distract	**15.** impact

SKILL DRILL 3

1. construct	**2.** spectators	**3.** vegetable	**4.** language	**5.** mileage
6. inspector	**7.** distract	**8.** compact	**9.** salvage	**10.** attract
11. managed	**12.** privilege	**13.** knowledge	**14.** wreckage	**15.** impact

SKILL DRILL 4

Order of answers may vary in 1–2, 6–9, 11–15.

1. inspector	**2.** spectators	**3.** vegetable	**4.** knowledge	**5.** privilege
6. attract	**7.** compact	**8.** distract	**9.** impact	**10.** construct
11. language	**12.** managed	**13.** mileage	**14.** salvage	**15.** wreckage

WORD GAME 13

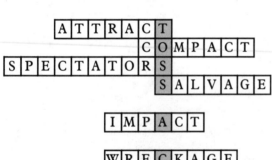

What did Maren Seidler's father tell her to do in order to see the world? *TOSS A CANNONBALL*

HOW WELL CAN YOU SPELL?

A. 1. wreckage   2. mileage   3. spectators   4. privilege   5. distract
6. inspector   7. impact   8. salvage

B. 9. compact   10. attracts   11. vegetable   12. language   13. construct
14. managed   15. knowledge

Additional Activities

In order to strengthen pronunciation and spelling skills, pair off students and allow one student to test the other on the "Study List" words.

Supplementary Words

budge	neglect	shortage
collect	patronage	sledge
destruct	pledge	smudge
detect	predict	submerge
garbage	punctuation	trudge
intellect	protection	

---

14. Andre

Pages 105–112

Objective

The purpose of this lesson is to focus on words that end in *ance*. Misspelling of these words is based primarily on pronunciation. The teacher should emphasize the difference in pronunciation of these words as opposed to the pronunciation of those that end in *ence*. See the following lesson for words ending in *ence*.

REVIEWING YOUR READING

1. c   2. b   3. a   4. c   5. b   6. d   7. b   8. b

FIGURING THE FACTS

Wording may vary for false answers.
1. T   2. T   3. F; harbor   4. F; likes   5. F; Atlantic Ocean   6. T   7. F; Statue   8. T   9. F; doing stunts   10. T

WHAT'S YOUR OPINION?

Answers will vary.

SKILL DRILL 1

1. insur(ance)   2. acquaint(ance)   3. ignor(ance)   4. perform(ance)   5. adv(ance)
6. appear(ance)   7. clear(ance)   8. accept(ance)   9. entr(ance)   10. import(ance)
11. remembr(ance)   12. allow(ance)   13. assist(ance)   14. dist(ance)   15. endur(ance)

SKILL DRILL 2

1. importance	**2.** insurance	**3.** performance	**4.** remembrance	**5.** advance
6. assistance	**7.** clearance	**8.** endurance	**9.** acceptance	**10.** distance
11. acquaintance	**12.** entrance	**13.** ignorance	**14.** allowance	**15.** appearance

SKILL DRILL 3

1. appearance	**2.** entrance	**3.** endurance	**4.** assistance	**5.** acquaintance
6. distance	**7.** remembrance	**8.** importance	**9.** insurance	**10.** performance
11. allowance	**12.** acceptance	**13.** advance	**14.** clearance	**15.** ignorance

SKILL DRILL 4

Order of answers may vary in 1–2.

1. endurance	**2.** entrance	**3.** insurance	**4.** distance	**5.** remembrance
6. advance	**7.** ignorance	**8.** appearance	**9.** assistance	**10.** importance
11. performance	**12.** acquaintance	**13.** allowance	**14.** acceptance	**15.** clearance

WORD GAME 14

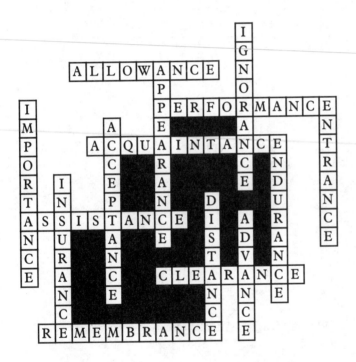

HOW WELL CAN YOU SPELL?

A. 1. ignorance   2. remembrance   3. clearance   4. allowance   5. acquaintance

     6. performance   7. assistance   8. appearance

B. 9. distance   10. acceptance   11. insurance   12. entrance   13. advance

     14. endurance   15. importance

See Lesson 15 for an additional activity.

15. Our Trace
Pages 113–120

Objective
This lesson deals with words ending in *ence*. The teacher should draw comparisons between the words that appear in Lesson 14 and the words in this lesson. Once again, pronunciation of these words should be stressed. It may be beneficial to overemphasize the differences at first, and then as the students begin to learn the words, pronounce them normally.

REVIEWING YOUR READING
1. b   2. c   3. d   4. a   5. b   6. c   7. d   8. a

FIGURING THE FACTS
1. F; a comedienne   2. T   3. T   4. F; an acting school   5. T   6. T
7. F; 4   8. F; Our Trace   9. T   10. T

WHAT'S YOUR OPINION?
Answers will vary.

SKILL DRILL 1
1. correspond(ence)   2. experi(ence)   3. comm(ence)   4. refer(ence)   5. abs(ence)
6. exist(ence)   7. differ(ence)   8. influ(ence)   9. confid(ence)   10. conveni(ence)
11. independ(ence)   12. audi(ence)   13. circumfer(ence)   14. coincid(ence)

SKILL DRILL 2
1. independence   2. convenience   3. coincidence   4. confidence   5. experience
6. difference   7. correspondence   8. commence   9. audience   10. circumference
11. existence   12. influence   13. absence   14. reference

SKILL DRILL 3
1. absence   2. influence   3. circumference   4. commence   5. confidence
6. difference   7. convenience   8. independence   9. coincidence   10. experience
11. correspondence   12. audience   13. existence

SKILL DRILL 4
Order of answers may vary in 1–2, 3–4, 11–12.
1. confidence   2. convenience   3. influence   4. independence   5. circumference
6. absence   7. reference   8. difference   9. correspondence   10. coincidence
11. existence   12. experience   13. commence   14. audience

WORD GAME 15

HOW WELL CAN YOU SPELL?

A. 1. existence 2. convenience 3. independence 4. reference 5. coincidence

6. circumference 7. correspondence 8. commence

B. 9. experience 10. absence 11. audience 12. confidence 13. independence

14. influence 15. difference

An Additional Activity

Have students make up a set of flash cards using the base part of the words listed in Lessons 14 and 15. Allow the students to drill one another on which ending should be used.

Optional Testing List

Lessons 11–15

absence

accomplice

advertise

advice

advise

ambitious

apprentice

approach

attract

audience

caution

ceiling

circumference

coincidence

commence

compact

confidence

construct

convenience

cooperate

correspondence

council

counsel

counterfeit

criticize

difference

disguise	patronize
distract	practice
except	prejudice
exercise	presence
existence	privilege
experience	proclaim
flair	realize
impact	reference
improvise	reliable
independence	revise
individual	salvage
influence	sealing
inspector	seen
itemize	serious
knowledge	splice
language	standardize
lieutenant	summarize
managed	vacuum
manual	valuable
mileage	vegetable
mourning	weather
nervous	

---

16. Tuned In

Pages 121–128

Objective

This lesson deals with *homophones*, or words that sound alike but have a different spelling and meaning. Homophones cause problems not only when misused but also when misspelled. It is most important that students understand the definitions of words involved. The "Skill Drills" and "Word Game" give practice in this area, but it may also be a good idea for the teacher to assign additional drill work.

REVIEWING YOUR READING
1. c   **2.** d   **3.** a   **4.** d   **5.** b   **6.** b   **7.** c   **8.** a

FIRST THINGS FIRST
1. Nam June Paik was born in Korea.
2. He moved to Japan at a young age.
3. As a boy in Japan he found the radio fascinating.
4. The invention of TV caused him to widen his interests.
5. He moved to Germany to study electronics.
6. Nam June composed electronic music.
7. Paik learned about radar waves.
8. He began to use televisions to make "electronic paintings."

WHAT'S YOUR OPINION?

Answers will vary.

SKILL DRILL 1

1. morning	2. ceiling	3. council	4. mourning	5. whether
6. counsel	7. ring	8. rap	9. scene	10. sealing
11. flair	12. seen	13. flare	14. weather	15. wrap
16. wring				

SKILL DRILL 2

1. scene	2. flair	3. council	4. sealing	5. flare
6. whether	7. seen	8. mourning	9. ceiling	10. wring
11. wrap	12. rap	13. ring	14. weather	15. counsel
16. morning				

SKILL DRILL 3

Order of answers may vary in 1–2, 5–6, 9–10, 11–16.

1. weather	2. whether	3. flair	4. flare	5. rap
6. wrap	7. seen	8. scene	9. council	10. counsel
11. ceiling	12. morning	13. mourning	14. ring	15. sealing
16. wring				

SKILL DRILL 4

1. mourning	2. counsel	3. sealing	4. ceiling	5. scene
6. flair	7. whether	8. flare	9. seen	10. weather
11. ring	12. council	13. wrap	14. rap	15. wring
16. morning				

WORD GAME 16

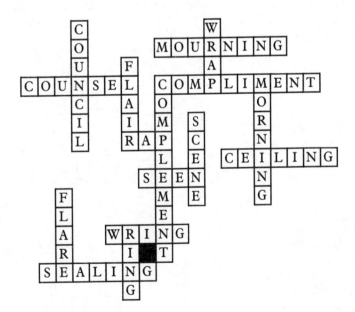

HOW WELL CAN YOU SPELL?

1. weather
2. flair
3. ceiling
4. council
5. counsel
6. seen
7. mourning
8. sealing
9. morning
10. whether
11. flare
12. ring
13. wring
14. wrap
15. scene
16. rap

An Additional Activity

Have students make up sentences to illustrate their knowledge of the homophones in this lesson. Ask students to check one another on the correct usage and spelling of each homophone.

Supplementary Words

accept—except
advice—advise
aloud—allowed
brake—break
cereal—serial
core—corps
flea—flee
hair—heir

hanger—hangar
mail—male
meddle—medal
meat—meet
pair—pear
peal—peel
tide—tied

---

17. Magnificent Marathon

Pages 129–136

Objective

The purpose of this lesson is to introduce four rules for *capitalization*. (a) Capitalize the first word in a sentence. (2) Capitalize the days of the week, months, and holidays. (3) Capitalize the names of people, titles, and the names of organizations. (4) Capitalize geographical terms or the names of places such as cities, states, countries, rivers, and oceans. The students should be made aware of the importance of capitalization in their written work. If a word is not capitalized and it should be, the word is spelled incorrectly.

REVIEWING YOUR READING

1. d   2. a   3. b   4. b   5. a   6. a   7. b   8. b

FIGURING THE FACTS

Wording may vary for false answers.

1. T   2. T   3. F; Candle of Understanding   4. F; not to continue   5. T
6. F; 6:00 A.M.   7. F; with her father   8. T   9. T   10. T

WHAT'S YOUR OPINION?

Answers will vary.

SKILL DRILL 1

1. (T)uesday
2. (W)ednesday
3. (A)tlantic (O)cean
4. (S)eptember
5. (N)ew (H)ampshire
6. (F)ourth of (J)uly
7. (J)une
8. (U)nited (S)tates
9. (A)rkansas
10. (C)alifornia
11. (M)ayor (C)hicado
12. (F)ebruary
13. (G)overnor (O)rebon
14. (N)iagara (F)alls
15. (L)abor (D)ay

SKILL DRILL 2

Order of answers may vary in 1–3, 4–5, 6–8, 10–11, 12–13, 14–15.

1. Arkansas
2. California
3. New Hampshire
4. Tuesday
5. Wednesday
6. February
7. June
8. September
9. United Nations
10. Governor Orebon
11. Mayor Chicado
12. Fourth of July
13. Labor Day
14. Atlantic Ocean
15. Niagara Falls or Arkansas, California, New Hampshire

SKILL DRILL 3

1. September
2. February
3. Niagara Falls
4. Atlantic Ocean
5. Labor Day
6. Fourth of July
7. Major Chicado
8. United Nations
9. June
10. Governor Orebon
11. Tuesday
12. Arkansas
13. Wednesday
14. New Hampshire
15. California

SKILL DRILL 4

1. September
2. United Nations
3. June
4. Tuesday
5. Arkansas
6. Wednesday
7. Governor Orebon
8. February
9. Niagara Falls
10. Atlantic Ocean
11. Labor Day
12. Fourth of July
13. Mayor Chicado
14. California
15. New Hampshire

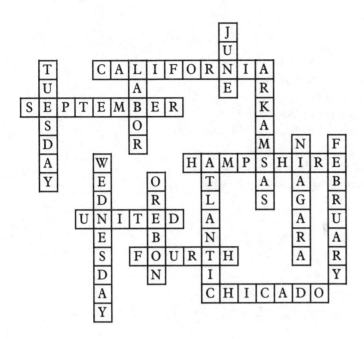

HOW WELL CAN YOU SPELL?

1. New Hampshire
2. September
3. United Nations
4. June
5. Tuesday
6. Arkansas
7. Wednesday
8 Governor
9. February
10. Niagara
11. Atlantic
12. Labor Day
13. Fourth
14. Mayor
15. California

An Additional Activity

Have students deliberately compose a paragraph without using any capitals. Then have the students swap papers and correct one another's work. Students get one point for every word that should be capitalized that their opponent has not found. The player with the most points wins.

Supplementary Words

Any proper nouns would be adequate for this lesson. Some of the most useful proper nouns for the students would be holidays and geographical terms.

18. Jaws and Claws

Pages 127–144

Objective

The objective of this lesson is to review the rules for capitalization that were introduced in Lesson 17, and to introduce two more rules for capitalization. The teacher should take this opportunity to reread the list of rules with the students and point out those that have already been learned. Then the teacher can emphasize the two new rules, which are: (1) Capitalize the names of languages or adjectives that describe the people from a certain country. (2) Capitalize the names of printed matter such as books, magazines, and newspapers. It would be wise to also review adjectives and their usage.

REVIEWING YOUR READING

1. b 2. a 3. c 4. c 5. d 6. b 7. a 8. a

FIGURING THE FACTS

Wording may vary for false answers.

1. T 2. F; can be 3. T 4. F; swamps 5. T 6. T 7. F; do have
8. T 9. T 10. F; mother

WHAT'S YOUR OPINION?

Answers will vary.

SKILL DRILL 1

1. (G)ermany 2. (U)niversity of (F)lorida 3. (T)hanksgiving 4. (T)hursday 5. (S)ports (I)llustrated

6. (A)ugust 7. (C)hinese 8. (E)gyptians 9. (N)ew (Y)ear's (D)ay 10. (S)panish

11. (R)ocky (M)ountains 12. (M)ississippi (R)iver 13. (T)he (S)carlet (L)etter 14. (C)atcher in the (R)ye 15. (L)ouisiana

SKILL DRILL 2

Order of answers may vary in 3-4, 5-6, 7-8, 9-11, 12-13.

1. Louisiana 2. Germany 3. Chinese 4. Spanish 5. Mississippi River

6. Rocky Mountains 7. New Year's Day 8. Thanksgiving 9. *Catcher in the Rye* 10. *Sports Illustrated*

11. *The Scarlet Letter* 12. August 13. Thursday 14. University of Florida 15. Egyptians

SKILL DRILL 3

1. Germany 2. Egyptians 3. August 4. Mississippi River 5. Thursday

6. *Catcher in the Rye* 7. *Sports Illustrated* 8. *The Scarlet Letter* 9. University of Florida 10. Rocky Mountains

11. Thanksgiving 12. Louisiana 13. Spanish 14. New Year's Day 15. Chinese

SKILL DRILL 4

1. *Sports Illustrated*
2. *Catcher in the Rye*
3. Thursday
4. Mississippi River
5. August
6. Egyptians
7. Germany
8. Chinese
9. New Year's Day
10. Spanish
11. Louisiana
12. Thanksgiving
13. Rocky Mountains
14. University of Florida
15. *The Scarlet Letter*

WORD GAME 18

HOW WELL CAN YOU SPELL?

1. University of Florida
2. *The Scarlet Letter*
3. Rocky Mountains
4. Thanksgiving
5. Louisiana
6. Spanish
7. New Year's Day
8. Chinese
9. Germany
10. Egyptians
11. August
12. Mississippi River
13. Thursday
14. *Sports Illustrated*
15. *Catcher in the Rye*

An Additional Activity

Have students make a list of examples that apply to each of the six rules. The student with the most examples wins.

Supplementary Words

Refer to Lesson 17.

19. Current Electricity

Pages 145–152

Objective

The purpose of this and the next lesson is to introduce a list of more difficult spelling words, commonly referred to as "spelling demons." At this time, the teacher should instruct the students in the use of memory devices in spelling. This may help students and give many a new outlook on their study skills. For example, if students have difficulty remembering that there are two *r*'s in *tomorrow*, they may choose to remember a phrase like *"tomorrow* there will be no *sorrow*," and recall the relationship between *tomorrow* and *sorrow*.

REVIEWING YOUR READING

1. b   **2.** a   **3.** d   **4.** a   **5.** a   **6.** c   **7.** c   **8.** a

FIGURING THE FACTS

Wording may vary for false answers.

1. F; center of the turbine   **2.** T   **3.** F; electricity   **4.** T   **5.** F; "yes"   **6.** F; 20 billion dollars   **7.** F; below the surface   **8.** T   **9.** T   **10.** F; are looking for

WHAT'S YOUR OPINION?

Answers will vary.

SKILL DRILL 1

1. pro(b)a(b)ly   **2.** responsib(ility)   **3.** o(cc)a(sion)   **4.** camp(aign)   **5.** tomo(rr)o(w)

6. (gu)arant(ee)   **7.** merchand(ise)   **8.** (vic)inity   **9.** prev(ious)   **10.** unu(sual)

11. u(nn)e(c)e(ss)ary   **12.** tremend(ous)   **13.** impo(ssible)   **14.** para(ll)el   **15.** thor(ough)ly

SKILL DRILL 2

1. merchandise   **2.** parallel   **3.** probably   **4.** thoroughly   **5.** vicinity

6. responsibility   **7.** tomorrow   **8.** occasion   **9.** unusual   **10.** campaign

11. unnecessary   **12.** previous   **13.** tremendous   **14.** guarantee   **15.** impossible

SKILL DRILL 3

1. unnecessary   **2.** unusual   **3.** tomorrow   **4.** guarantee   **5.** parallel

6. probably   **7.** vicinity   **8.** previous   **9.** campaign   **10.** tremendous

11. impossible   **12.** merchandise   **13.** thoroughly   **14.** responsibility   **15.** occasion

SKILL DRILL 4

Order of answers may vary in 1–2, 3–4, 6–7.

1. vicinity   **2.** responsibility   **3.** tremendous   **4.** previous   **5.** thoroughly

6. impossible   **7.** unnecessary   **8.** occasion   **9.** campaign   **10.** unusual

11. parallel   **12.** probably   **13.** guarantee   **14.** merchandise   **15.** tomorrow

WORD GAME 19

What are scientists looking for? *ENERGY*

HOW WELL CAN YOU SPELL?

A. 1. vicinity   2. tremendous   3. thoroughly   4. unnecessary   5. occasion

      6. parallel   7. probably   8. guarantee

B. 9. impossible   10. campaign   11. unusual   12. merchandise   13. tomorrow

      14. responsibility   15. previous

An Additional Activity

Have students take the "Study List" words and make up their own memory devices for the spelling of each word. Ask them to write their devices down and read them to the class. The teacher may want to take the best device for each word, make a comprehensive list for the "Study List" words, and hand them out to the class.

Supplementary Words

accident	benefit	disastrous
accommodate	century	politician
acquaint	challenge	roommate
adolescent	column	scenery
advantageous	correspondence	shepherd
advisable	defenseless	syllable

---

20. The Haunted Jewel

Pages 153–160

Objective

As in the previous lesson, the focus here is on "spelling demons." The teacher should review the "Study List" words with the students, pointing out the difficult spots in each. The "Skill Drills" will help in doing this, but the difficulty of the words makes it necessary to give this list special attention.

REVIEWING YOUR READING

1. c   2. a   3. d   4. b   5. b   6. d   7. b   8. c

FIGURING THE FACTS

Wording may vary for false answers.

1. T   2. F; blue   3. F; beheaded   4. T   5. F; penniless   6. F; an actress

7. T   8. F; first   9. F; necklace   10. T

WHAT'S YOUR OPINION?

Answers will vary.

SKILL DRILL 1

1. sep(a)rate
2. su(ccee)d
3. lon(e)liness
4. pu(n)ctuation
5. reco(mm)end
6. vit(a)min
7. prefe(rr)ed
8. stra(igh)ten
9. di(a)mond
10. po(ss)e(ss)
11. rum(or)
12. statu(e)
13. int(e)rpret
14. med(i)cine
15. proc(ee)d

SKILL DRILL 2

1. rumor
2. statue
3. interpret
4. medicine
5. separate
6. succeed
7. diamond
8. loneliness
9. possess
10. punctuation
11. recommend
12. vitamin
13. preferred
14. proceed
15. straighten

SKILL DRILL 3

1. separate
2. recommend
3. interpret
4. diamond
5. preferred
6. loneliness
7. rumor
8. succeed
9. statue
10. medicine
11. vitamin
12. proceed
13. straighten
14. possess
15. punctuation

SKILL DRILL 4

Order of answers may vary in 2–3.

1. punctuation
2. proceed
3. succeed
4. recommend
5. separate
6. interpret
7. statue
8. possess
9. loneliness
10. rumor
11. preferred
12. diamond
13. medicine
14. vitamin
15. straighten

WORD GAME 20

HOW WELL CAN YOU SPELL?

A.
1. recommend
2. interpret
3. statue
4. possess
5. loneliness
6. straighten
7. separate
8 punctuation

B.
9. proceed
10. preferred
11. vitamin
12. succeed
13. medicine
14. diamond
15. rumor

An Additional Activity

Have students make lists of their own personal "spelling demons," or those words that they consider more difficult to spell. It may be helpful to use the "Mini-Dictionary" in the back of the text.

Supplementary Words

customary	experiment
cylinder	explanation
dangerous	excellent
descent	exhibit
desperate	families
discuss	healthy
disease	interpretation
divide	jewelry
either	leisurely
emptiness	literature
enormous	loyalty

Optional Testing List

Lessons 16–20

acceptance	Niagara Falls
acquaintance	occasion
allowance	parallel
appearance	performance
Arkansas	preferred
assistance	probably
Atlantic Ocean	proceed
August	punctuation
California	recommend
campaign	remembrance
clearance	responsibility
Egyptians	Rocky Mountains
endurance	separate
February	September
guarantee	*Sports Illustrated*
ignorance	statue
importance	straighten
insurance	succeed
interpret	Thanksgiving
Labor Day	thoroughly
loneliness	tommorrow
Louisiana	tremendous
merchandise	United Nations
Mississippi River	unnecessary
New Hampshire	unusual
New Year's Day	vicinity

Spell It Out—Book 4:
Sample Lesson Plan

Roseanne

Pages 1–8

Objectives

• To learn three rules of pluralization: (1) Add *s* to the singular form. (2) Add *es* to words ending in *ch* or *sh*. (3) For nouns ending in *y* preceded by a consonant, change the *y* to *i* before adding *es*.

• To improve the reading skills of finding the main idea, remembering details, vocabulary development, and making inferences.

Motivation

For this lesson, begin with a discussion of Roseanne Barr's television show. Ask whether any students have seen the show. Why did they like or dislike it? Ask whether anyone knows about Roseanne's private life.

Procedure

1. Ask questions about the opening picture. Who is in the photo? What is she doing, or what might she be doing? What does the photo tell about her?

2. Have the students read the story silently. Instruct them to turn the page and complete the "Reviewing Your Reading" and "Figuring the Facts" exercises. Slower students might find it necessary to reread the selection before completing the "Figuring the Facts" exercise.

3. Choose students to go back and read the story aloud. Then ask individual students to read and answer the questions orally. This will provide a group activity and an answer check for all students.

4. Direct the students to answer the "What's Your Opinion?" exercise. This section may be used as a discussion activity, a writing activity, or both. Students may write their answers, then read them aloud. They may also discuss the differences in their answers. Since the student answers will vary, they will not appear in the Answer Key that follows.

5. Have students turn to the "Developing Spelling Skills" section. Explain that the words in the "Study List" demonstrate the particular rules or patterns that are discussed in the spelling lesson. The text will help you to explain the spelling rules. The teacher should also review each of the "Study List" words with the students, explaining the pluralization of each and reviewing the meaning. Instruct the students to refer to the "Mini-Dictionary" (page 162) to find definitions of any words they are unsure of.

6. Direct the students to begin the series of "Skill Drills." In some of the exercises, students may list their answers in any order; however, the Answer Key lists the words alphabetically, where applicable, for your convenience.

7. After the "Skill Drills" and the "Word Game" have been completed and checked, direct the students to complete "How Well Can You Spell?" a review quiz. You might want to have the students check their own work while you read the correct answers aloud. This can be especially reinforcing because the students have the opportunity to correct their own errors and strengthen their own knowledge of the words.

Follow-Up

1. Have the students do research in recent periodicals on Roseanne Barr and prepare a short written report.

2. Have students prepare a notebook to catalog the spelling rules and words that exemplify each rule.

3. Have students keep a list of all words that they have misspelled in their writing. The student should copy the misspelled word, circle the error, and then write the word correctly. This error analysis can be quite beneficial in learning correct spellings.

4. Where possible, have students substitute the "Challenge Words" in the exercises, writing definitions, pluralizing the words, circling any confusing letter combinations, and using the words in sentences.

Spell It Out—Book 4:
Manual and Answer Key

1. Roseanne

Pages 1–8

Objective

The object of this lesson is to review some of the most frequently used rules for pluralization: adding *s* to the singular form; adding *es* to words that end in *ch* or *sh;* and pluralizing words that end in *y* preceded by a consonant. Each of these concepts has been previously introduced in lower levels of the *Spell It Out* series, and students should already be familiar with them. The teacher should explain each rule, emphasizing that the "Study List" words serve as models for hundreds of other nouns that form their plurals similarly.

Particular attention should be paid to the rule stating that words ending in *y* preceded by a consonant change the *y* to *i* before adding *es.* In *Spell It Out*—Book 1, this rule was taught in two sections: words ending in *y* preceded by a vowel (Lesson 18), and words ending in *y* preceded by a consonant (Lesson 19). For review purposes, we ask students to remember that the rule applies only to words ending in *y* preceded by a consonant. To emphasize this, the teacher should demonstrate that words ending in *y* preceded by a vowel form their plural by simply adding *s.* Typical examples include the following words: *essay, attorney, journey, turkey, display, valley, alley, and chimney.*

REVIEWING YOUR READING

1. a   **2.** c   **3.** a   **4.** d   **5.** b   **6.** d   **7.** b   **8.** c

FIGURING THE FACTS

1. T   **2.** T   **3.** F   **4.** F   **5.** F   **6.** T   **7.** T   **8.** F   **9.** T
10. F

WHAT'S YOUR OPINION?

Answers will vary.

SKILL DRILL 1

1. copies   **2.** melodies   **3.** personalities   **4.** stitches   **5.** autographs
6. wrenches   **7.** chocolates   **8.** ceremonies   **9.** opportunities   **10.** sandwiches
11. territories   **12.** cafeterias   **13.** vocalists   **14.** celebrities

SKILL DRILL 2

1. charity	2. ceremony	3. opportunity	4. vocalists	5. stitch
6. celebrities	7. copy	8. cafeterias	9. autograph	10. territory
11. wrenches	12. personality	13. sandwich	14. melodies	15. chocolates

SKILL DRILL 3

1. personalities	2. sandwiches	3. territories	4. wrenches	5. cafeterias
6. charities	7. ceremonies	8. opportunities	9. stitches	10. vocalists
11. autographs	12. celebrities	13. chocolates	14. melodies	15. copies

SKILL DRILL 4

copies	autographs	ceremony	personalities
wrenches	vocalist	cafeteria	chocolates
melody	celebrity	opportunity	sandwiches
stitches	territory	charity	

WORD GAME 1

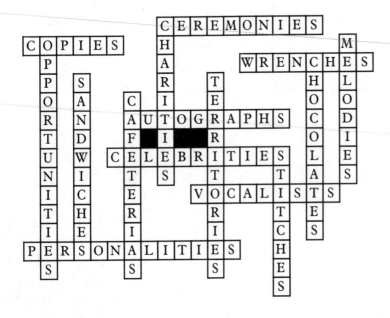

HOW WELL CAN YOU SPELL?

A.
1. cafeterias	2. ceremony	3. chocolate	4. personalities	5. stitches
6. wrenches	7. sandwiches			

B.
8. autographs	9. celebrities	10. charities	11. copies	12. opportunities
13. territories	14. vocalists	15. melodies		

2. Home on the Range

Objective

In this lesson, the emphasis is once again on rules for pluralization. As in the previous lesson, this is mainly a review of concepts that have been covered in other levels of *Spell It Out*. For specific levels and lessons, please consult the Scope and Sequence for the *Spell It Out* series.

The rule for pluralizing nouns that end in *o* preceded by a consonant is perhaps the most confusing of those presented in this lesson because there are several exceptions to the rule. The teacher should review the "Study List" with the class in order to draw attention to the exceptions. (The "Challenge Words" at the end of the lesson also contain some exceptions to this rule.) For accurate spelling, practice and application are more important than memorization of the rule. The teacher should stress this fact to the students when introducing the lesson.

REVIEWING YOUR READING

1. a   2. c   3. c   4. b   5. b   6. d   7. b   8. b

FIGURING THE FACTS

Wording may vary for false answers.

1. T   2. F; million   3. T   4. F; bison   5. T   6. T   7. T
8. T   9. F; lands   10. T

WHAT'S YOUR OPINION?

Answers will vary.

SKILL DRILL 1

1. spaghetti	2. portfolios	3. buffaloes	4. belief	5. volcanoes
6. tomatoes	7. mementos	8. species	9. mosquitoes	10. Eskimos
11. yourselves	12. thieves	13. tornadoes	14. kangaroos	15. handkerchiefs

SKILL DRILL 2

1. volcano	2. kangaroo	3. Eskimos	4. buffalo	5. handkerchief
6. tornadoes	7. tomato	8. thief	9. species	10. spaghetti
11. portfolios	12. mementos	13. mosquitoes	14. yourself	15. belief

SKILL DRILL 3

1. yourselves	2. tornadoes	3. thieves	4. spaghetti	5. mosquitoes
6. kangaroos	7. beliefs	8. volcanoes	9. tomatoes	10. species
11. portfolios	12. mementos	13. handkerchiefs	14. Eskimos	15. buffaloes

SKILL DRILL 4

Order of answers may vary in 1–5, 6–7, 8–9, 10–11, 12–13.

1. buffaloes
2. mosquitoes
3. tomatoes
4. tornadoes
5. volcanoes
6. thieves
7. yourselves
8. spaghetti
9. species
10. kangaroo
11. portfolio
12. beliefs
13. handkerchiefs
14. Eskimos
15. mementos

WORD GAME 2

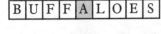

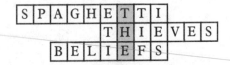

What has the bison finally found? *A HOME ON THE RANGE*

HOW WELL CAN YOU SPELL?

A.
1. Eskimos
2. beliefs
3. mementoes
4. mosquitoes
5. species
6. thieves
7. volcanoes
8. yourselves

B.
9. buffaloes
10. handkerchiefs
11. kangaroos
12. portfolios
13. spaghetti
14. tomatoes
15. tornadoes

---

3. La Cantadora

Pages 17–24

Objective

This lesson deals with words that have the vowel combination *ie* or *ei*. The familiar *i before e* rule is explained and discussed. Students should commit this rule to memory, as it is often helpful. The "Study List" not only contains words that adhere to the rule, but also the exceptions. Memorization of a "list" of exceptions is not recommended, as each word is an exception for a particular reason. However, memorization of each individual spelling is imperative. The most productive method of learning these difficult spellings is to use these words in writing. The teacher should assign activities that stress this type of practice.

REVIEWING YOUR READING

1. c   **2.** b   **3.** c   **4.** d   **5.** a   **6.** b   **7.** a   **8.** a

FIGURING THE FACTS

Wording may vary for false answers.

1. F; singer   **2.** T   **3.** F; not   **4.** F; bands which played at weddings (marriages)
5. F; not very well   **6.** T   **7.** T   **8.** T   **9.** T   **10.** T

WHAT'S YOUR OPINION?

Answers will vary.

SKILL DRILL 1

1. suffic(ie)nt	**2.** effic(ie)nt	**3.** consc(ie)nce	**4.** anc(ie)nt	**5.** b(ei)ge
6. r(ei)gning	**7.** n(ei)ghborhood	**8.** rec(ei)ved	**9.** dec(ei)ve	**10.** conc(ei)ted
11. ach(ie)vement	**12.** exper(ie)nce	**13.** hyg(ie)ne	**14.** forf(ei)t	**15.** counterf(ei)t

SKILL DRILL 2

1. neighborhood	**2.** beige	**3.** ancient	**4.** sufficient	**5.** received
6. reigning	**7.** counterfeit	**8.** forfeit	**9.** deceive	**10.** efficient
11. conscience	**12.** experience	**13.** hygiene	**14.** conceited	**15.** achievement

SKILL DRILL 3

1. hygiene	**2.** ancient	**3.** achievement	**4.** conscience	**5.** received
6. conceited	**7.** efficient	**8.** forfeit	**9.** beige	**10.** counterfeit
11. sufficient	**12.** reigning	**13.** deceive	**14.** experience	**15.** neighborhood

SKILL DRILL 4

Order of answers may vary in 1–3, 4–7, 8–10, 11–13, 14–15.

1. received	**2.** conceited	**3.** deceive	**4.** ancient	**5.** efficient
6. conscience	**7.** sufficient	**8.** beige	**9.** neighborhood	**10.** reigning
11. hygiene	**12.** experience	**13.** achievement	**14.** forfeit	**15.** counterfeit

WORD GAME 3

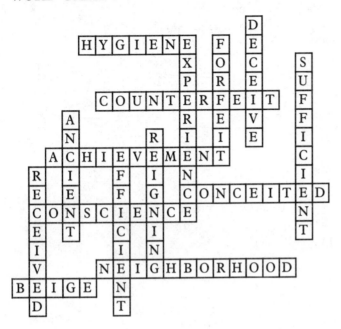

HOW WELL CAN YOU SPELL?

A. 1. neighborhood 2. achievement 3. conceited 4. deceive 5. efficient
6. received 7. conscience

B. 8. reigning 9. experience 10. ancient 11. counterfeit 12. hygiene
13. forfeit 14. beige 15. sufficient

---

4. Bill Cosby's Helpful Hints

Pages 25–32

Objective

The focus of this lesson is on reviewing three spelling rules that deal with adding a *suffix*. The teacher should emphasize that a suffix is a word part that is added to the end of a word and give some examples of different types of suffixes. The three rules outlined in the lesson are related, in that they deal with doubling or not doubling the final consonant in a word when adding a suffix. The teacher would be wise to point out the similarities in the rules by demonstrating that the final consonant is doubled only if the word ends in a single consonant preceded by a single vowel and the suffix begins with a vowel.

REVIEWING YOUR READING

1. b   2. b   3. b   4. b   5. c   6. a   7. c   8. b

FIGURING THE FACTS

Wording may vary for false answers.

1. T   2. T   3. T   4. F; sometimes   5. T   6. F; light reading
7. F; general idea   8. T   9. F; is   10. T

WHAT'S YOUR OPINION?

Answers will vary.

SKILL DRILL 1

1. permitted	2. suggestion	3. referred	4. admitted	5. compelled
6. occurred	7. controlled	8. transferred	9. revealed	10. handicapped
11. committed	12. equipped	13. previewing	14. consulted	15. recommendation

SKILL DRILL 2

1. handicapped	2. controllable	3. consulted	4. compelled	5. committed
6. equipped	7. admitted	8. transferred	9. suggestion	10. occurred
11. permitted	12. revealed	13. previewing	14. recommendation	15. referred

SKILL DRILL 3

1. occurred	2. equipped	3. referred	4. consulted	5. committed
6. transferred	7. revealed	8. handicapped	9. previewing	10. controllable
11. compelled	12. admitted	13. suggestion	14. referred	15. recommendation

SKILL DRILL 4

previewed	previewing	permit	permitting
suggest	suggested	referred	referring
occur	occurring	handicap	handicapped
admitted	admitting	commit	committing
control	controlled	compelled	compelling
consult	consulting	reveal	revealed
transferred	transferring	recommend	recommending
equip	equipped		

WORD GAME 4

HOW WELL CAN YOU SPELL?

A.
1. permitted
2. committed
3. compelled
4. controllable
5. handicapped
6. revealed
7. transferred

B.
8. consulted
9. admitted
10. previewing
11. recommen-dation
12. referred
13. suggestion
14. occurred
15. equipped

---

5. What Goes Up

Pages 33–40

Objective

The focus of this lesson is on illustrating the rule stating that when a word ends in *y* preceded by a consonant, we change the *y* to *i* before adding any suffix except *ing*. The teacher should stress the second half of the rule, which states that when a word ends in *y* preceded by a vowel, the word remains unchanged when a suffix is added.

This rule is an extension of the rule stated in Lesson 1, which applies to pluralization. In this lesson, we are not only changing verb forms by adding suffixes, but also pluralizing nouns (as in Lesson 1). The object is to emphasize the fact that words ending in *y* require special attention and knowledge of the rules, regardless of whether they are verbs or nouns. The teacher should point this out to the class by noting the appropriate similarities.

REVIEWING YOUR READING

1. c   2. b   3. a   4. d   5. a   6. c   7. a   8. d

FIGURING THE FACTS

Wording may vary for false answers.

1. T   2. F; no one knows who the first jugglers were   3. T   4. T   5. F; still
6. T   7. T   8. T   9. F; an hour   10. F; 11

WHAT'S YOUR OPINION?

Answers will vary.

SKILL DRILL 1

1. groceries	2. libraries	3. replied	4. denied	5. notified
6. dismayed	7. liquefying	8. anniversaries	9. modified	10. qualified
11. simplifies	12. dictionaries	13. hurrying	14. portrayed	15. delayed

SKILL DRILL 2

1. liquefying	2. anniversaries	3. groceries	4. replied	5. simplifies
6. notified	7. libraries	8. hurrying	9. dictionaries	10. portrayed
11. denied	12. delayed	13. dismayed	14. qualified	15. modified

SKILL DRILL 3

1. portraying	2. dictionaries	3. groceries	4. liquefied	5. delaying
6. dismayed	7. relied	8. simplifying	9. hurried	10. modifying
11. denying	12. qualifying	13. notifying	14. libraries	15. anniversaries

SKILL DRILL 4

delay	delaying	dismaying	dismays
portrayed	portrays	denied	denies
hurried	hurrying	liquefying	liquefies
modified	modifies	notified	notifying
qualifying	qualifies	replied	replies
simplified	simplifying		

WORD GAME 5

```
                    D           N
              L     I           O
        L I B R A R I E S       T
              Q     M O D I F I E D
   Q          U     A           F
   U     D    S I M P L I F I E S I
   A     C    E     Y           E D
   L     T    Y     D           D
   I     I    I           P
   F     O    N         G R O C E R I E S
   I     N    G         R   O
   E     D              E   R
   D E L A Y E D        P   T
         E    A         L   R
         N    R     H U R R Y I N G
         I    I     E P   A
         E    S     L I   Y
   A N N I V E R S A R I E S
         D    S     E D   E
              D     D     D
```

HOW WELL CAN YOU SPELL?

A. 1. anniversaries   2. hurrying   3. libraries   4. liquefying   5. modified
     6. qualified   7. replied

B. 8. notified   9. portrayed   10. dictionaries
     11. denied   12. dismayed   13. groceries   14. delayed   15. simplifies

Optional Testing List

Lessons 1–5 (Challenge words are italicized.)

achievement	ceremonies	denied
admitted	ceremony	*deterred*
agencies	charities	dictionaries
ancient	charity	*disbelief*
anniversaries	chocolate(s)	dismayed
anxieties	committed	*echoes*
assemblies	compelled	efficient
autograph(s)	conceited	*embargoes*
avocados	*conferred*	embassies
beige	conscience	*emitting*
belief(s)	consulted	equipped
broccoli	controllable	Eskimo(s)
buffalo(es)	copies	*excelling*
cafeteria(s)	copy	experience
celebrities	counterfeit	*falsifying*
celebrity	deceive	forfeit
centuries	delayed	*grievance*

groceries	*personality*	stitch(es)
handicapped	portfolio(s)	sufficient
handkerchief(s)	portrayed	suggestion
heroes	previewing	*surveillance*
hurrying	*priorities*	*symphonies*
hygiene	*propelled*	territories
identities	qualified	territory
intensified	*rebelled*	*testimonies*
kangaroo(s)	received	*theories*
leisurely	recommendation	thief
libraries	referred	thieves
liquefying	*regretted*	tomato(es)
masterpiece	reigning	tornado(es)
melodies	*remedies*	transferred
melody	*remitting*	*tuxedos*
memento(s)	replied	*unforgettable*
modified	revealed	*universities*
mosquito(es)	*salmon*	*unveil*
neighborhood	sandwich(es)	*verified*
notified	*sheriffs*	vocalist(s)
occurred	*shrieking*	volcano(s)
opportunities	*signifying*	wrench(es)
opportunity	simplifies	*wristwatches*
perceive	sopranos	*yield*
permitted	spaghetti	yourself
personalities	species	yourselves
	specified	

---

6. Over Easy

Pages 41–48

Objective

This lesson focuses on words containing letters that are not sounded when the word is pronounced. In the *Spell It Out* series, we refer to these as "silent letters." By emphasizing these as silent letters, the student will be more apt to focus on this often misspelled part of the word and will be able to make generalizations about similar words.

It may be of some help for the student to pronounce these silent letters when memorizing the spelling of the word. Some researchers have found that when students deliberately mispronounce words while learning to spell them, they get a more meaningful mental impression of the accurate spelling. For example, when studying the spelling of the word *often*, the student is more apt to remember that there is a silent *t* if he or she mentally pronounces the word as *of/TEN*. However, the teacher should make it clear that this is not how the word is pronounced in everyday conversation.

REVIEWING YOUR READING

1. c   **2.** b   **3.** d   **4.** c   **5.** c   **6.** a   **7.** b   **8.** a

FIGURING THE FACTS

Wording may vary for false answers.

1. F; and   **2.** T   **3.** F; about the size of a softball   **4.** F; about 12   **5.** T
6. F; many more   **7.** T   **8.** F; about the size of   **9.** T   **10.** T

WHAT'S YOUR OPINION?

Answers will vary.

SKILL DRILL 1

1. numer(o)us   **2.** forei(g)ner   **3.** fas(c)inating   **4.** tong(ue)   **5.** s(c)i(s)sors
6. smu(d)ge   **7.** ans(w)er(e)d   **8.** g(u)arante(e)   **9.** r(h)yme   **10.** of(t)en
11. s(c)enery   **12.** r(h)ythm   **13.** (a)i(s)le   **14.** stomac(h)   **15.** ac(k)no(w)le(d)ge

SKILL DRILL 2

1. scissors   **2.** foreigner   **3.** tongue   **4.** stomach   **5.** smudge
6. answered   **7.** fascinating   **8.** numerous   **9.** scenery   **10.** rhyme
11. rhythm   **12.** guarantee   **13.** acknowledge   **14.** aisle   **15.** often

SKILL DRILL 3

1. tongue   **2.** smudge   **3.** scenery   **4.** acknowledge   **5.** answered
6. foreigner   **7.** guarantee   **8.** stomach   **9.** scissors   **10.** rhythm
11. aisle   **12.** often   **13.** fascinating   **14.** numerous   **15.** rhyme

SKILL DRILL 4

Order of answers may vary in 1–2, 3–5, 6–7

1. acknowledge   **2.** smudge   **3.** scissors   **4.** fascinating   **5.** scenery
6. rhyme   **7.** rhythm   **8.** often   **9.** stomach   **10.** foreigner
11. aisle   **12.** numerous   **13.** guarantee   **14.** tongue   **15.** answered

WORD GAME 6

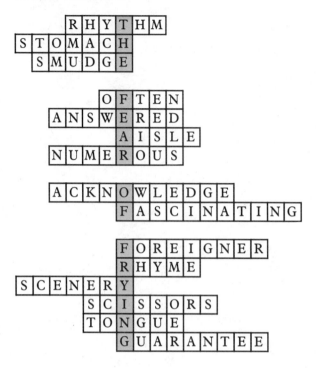

What do you get when you put on your gear and enter a flying chamber? *THE FEAR OF FRYING*

HOW WELL CAN YOU SPELL?

A. 1. numerous   2. rhyme   3. smudge   4. acknowledge   5. fascinating
     6. foreigner   7. tongue

B. 8. stomach   9. aisle   10. answered   11. rhythm   12. scenery
     13. scissors   14. guarantee   15. often

---

7. Food for Thought
Pages 49–56

Objective

The object of this lesson is to demonstrate how the letter *u* is used in combination with other vowels to spell different sounds. The focus is on spelling the long *u* sound in words like *pursuit* and *tissue*. The lesson also examines words that have the short *i* sound or the long *i* sound spelled *ui*, as in *biscuit* and *disguise*. Emphasis on the *ui* or *ue* combination in each "Study List" word should be stressed, as this combination is very often confused by students in their spelling.

REVIEWING YOUR READING

  1. b   2. c   3. a   4. c   5. a   6. d   7. c   8. b

FIGURING THE FACTS

Wording may vary for false answers.

1. T   2. T   3. F; 3 pounds   4. T   5. T   6. T   7. T
8. F; always   9. T   10. T

WHAT'S YOUR OPINION?

Answers will vary.

SKILL DRILL 1

1. tiss(ue)   2. purs(ui)t   3. g(ui)lty   4. discontin(ue)   5. resid(ue)
6. n(ui)sance   7. fr(ui)tful   8. resc(ue)   9. j(ui)ciest   10. exq(ui)site
11. bisc(ui)ts   12. q(ui)lted   13. g(ui)tar   14. disg(ui)se   15. circ(ui)t

SKILL DRILL 2

1. pursuit   2. rescue   3. guitar   4. guilty   5. fruitful
6. discontinue   7. circuit   8. biscuits   9. disguise   10. exquisite
11. juiciest   12. nuisance   13. tissue   14. residue   15. quilted

SKILL DRILL 3

1. residue   2. nuisance   3. fruitful   4. discontinue   5. circuit
6. guilty   7. pursuit   8. quilted   9. guitar   10. exquisite
11. biscuits   12. disguise   13. juiciest   14. rescue   15. tissue

SKILL DRILL 4

Order of answers may vary in 1–4, 5–8, 9–14.

1. residue   2. rescue   3. discontinue   4. tissue   5. pursuit
6. nuisance   7. juiciest   8. fruitful   9. circuit   10. biscuits
11. guitar   12. guilty   13. exquisite   14. quilted   15. disguise

WORD GAME 7

HOW WELL CAN YOU SPELL?

A. **1.** circuit   **2.** fruitful   **3.** pursuit   **4.** quilted   **5.** residue

     6. rescue   **7.** juiciest

B. **8.** tissue   **9.** nuisance   **10.** guitar   **11.** guilty   **12.** exquisite

     13. discontinue   **14.** disguise   **15.** biscuits

---

8. Tackling Art

Pages 57–64

Objective

In this lesson, the focus is on various ways that the *sh* sound is spelled: *sh*, *ci*, *ti*, and *ssi*. These different spellings are often confused by students in their writing. When the "Study List" words are memorized, they will serve as models for other words with similar spellings.

REVIEWING YOUR READING

1. c   **2.** d   **3.** a   **4.** b   **5.** b   **6.** b   **7.** b   **8.** b

FIGURING THE FACTS

Wording may vary for false answers.

1. T   **2.** T   **3.** F; wasn't used to   **4.** F; weightlifting   **5.** T   **6.** T

7. F; football   **8.** T   **9.** T   **10.** F; artist

WHAT'S YOUR OPINION?

Answers will vary.

SKILL DRILL 1

Order of answers may vary in 1–2, 3–8, 9–11, 12–15.

1. vanished
2. friendship
3. artificial
4. musician
5. politician
6. financial
7. official
8. special
9. graduation
10. transition
11. initial
12. session
13. discussion
14. professional
15. procession

SKILL DRILL 2

1. official
2. vanished
3. procession
4. politician
5. artificial
6. discussion
7. musician
8. special
9. financial
10. friendship
11. graduation
12. initial
13. professional
14. transition
15. session

SKILL DRILL 3

1. discussion
2. friendship
3. politician
4. session
5. artificial
6. graduation
7. professional
8. initial
9. official
10. procession
11. special
12. financial
13. musician
14. transition
15. vanished

SKILL DRILL 4

Order of answers may vary in 1–5, 6–11, 14–15.

1. discussion
2. session
3. graduation
4. transition
5. procession
6. artificial
7. official
8. financial
9. professional
10. initial
11. special
12. friendship
13. vanished
14. musician
15. politician

WORD GAME 8

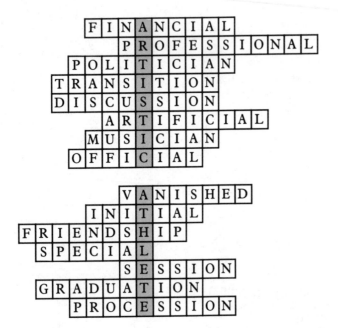

How could you describe Ernie Barnes? He's an *ARTISTIC ATHLETE.*

124

HOW WELL CAN YOU SPELL?

A.
1. official
2. professional
3. artificial
4. discussion
5. politician
6. session
7. transition

B.
8. friendship
9. graduation
10. initial
11. vanished
12. special
13. procession
14. financial
15. musician

---

9. Frozen Secrets

Pages 65–72

Objective

The focus of this lesson is on the long *i* and short *i* sounds spelled with the letter *y*. The teacher should supplement the examples in the text with other words that contain the long and short *i* sounds; for example, *miser, lightning, frighten, mitten, Indian,* and *violin*. Once the student is clear about which sound is which, the teacher should compare the spellings of these words with those in the "Study List," emphasizing that the list words have long and short i spelled with y instead of i.

As noted in the text, the list word *synonym* has two *y*'s, each sounding like a short *i*. The word *mythology* also contains two *y*'s, but the second makes the sound of long *e*.

REVIEWING YOUR READING

1. c
2. b
3. a
4. b
5. a
6. c
7. a
8. b

FIGURING THE FACTS

Wording may vary for false answers
1. T
2. T
3. T
4. F; plants
5. F; waves
6. T
7. F; does not have
8. F; solidifies
9. T
10. F; arm

WHAT'S YOUR OPINION?

Answers will vary.

SKILL DRILL 1

1. c(y)linder
2. enc(y)clopedia
3. s(y)non(y)m
4. s(y)nthetic
5. m(y)sterious
6. h(y)drogen
7. anton(y)m
8. cr(y)stals
9. t(y)phoon
10. s(y)mpathetic
11. solidif(y)
12. h(y)phen
13. g(y)mnasium
14. m(y)tholog(y)
15. s(y)mbolic

SKILL DRILL 2

1. mythology
2. solidify
3. sympathetic
4. crystals
5. antonym
6. synonym
7. encyclopedia
8. hydrogen
9. hyphen
10. typhoon
11. synthetic
12. symbolic
13. gymnasium
14. mysterious
15. cylinder

SKILL DRILL 3

1. typhoon
2. synonym
3. symbolic
4. mythology
5. hyphen
6. gymnasium
7. crystals
8. synthetic
9. sympathetic
10. solidify
11. mysterious
12. hydrogen
13. encyclopedia
14. cylinder
15. antonym

SKILL DRILL 4

Order of answers may vary in 1–2, 3–5, 6–7, 11–12.

1. typhoon
2. hyphen
3. symbolic
4. sympathetic
5. synthetic
6. synonym
7. antonym
8. mythology
9. gymnasium
10. solidify
11. cylinder
12. encyclopedia
13. mysterious
14. hydrogen
15. crystals

WORD GAME 9

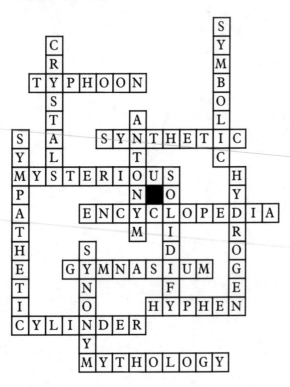

HOW WELL CAN YOU SPELL?

A.
1. cylinder
2. synthetic
3. solidify
4. mysterious
5. gymnasium
6. symbolic
7. encyclopedia

B.
8. mythology
9. hyphen
10. hydrogen
11. antonym
12. synonym
13. sympathetic
14. typhoon
15. crystals

10. Forever Friends

Pages 73–80

Objectives

This lesson examines words that have the *el* sound spelled *le* or *al* at the end of a word. Although there are other ways to spell this sound, students often find the *le* and *al* confusing. The method of pronouncing the spelling when memorizing the word is most appropriate for this lesson. For example, a student is more apt to remember the correct spelling of the word *article,* if he or she mentally pronounces the word as *ar/ti/CLE* (making the sound of long *e*). However, the teacher should point out that this pronunciation is for memorization purposes only, not for normal conversation.

REVIEWING YOUR READING

1. b   **2.** c   **3.** d   **4.** c   **5.** a   **6.** c   **7.** d   **8.** b

FIGURING THE FACTS

Wording may vary for false answers.

1. T   **2.** T   **3.** T   **4.** F; largest   **5.** F; Canadian   **6.** T
7. F; Canada   **8.** T   **9.** T   **10.** F; the same continent

WHAT'S YOUR OPINION?

Answers will vary.

SKILL DRILL 1

1. surviv(al)   **2.** simp(le)   **3.** season(al)   **4.** artic(le)   **5.** doub(le)
6. person(al)   **7.** fragi(le)   **8.** spectac(le)   **9.** sever(al)   **10.** rehears(al)
11. commerci(al)   **12.** receptac(le)   **13.** missi(le)   **14.** economic(al)   **15.** fiction(al)

SKILL DRILL 2

1. double   **2.** fragile   **3.** several   **4.** fictional   **5.** rehearsal
6. seasonal   **7.** spectacle   **8.** receptacle   **9.** missile   **10.** article
11. commercial   **12.** economical   **13.** simple   **14.** survival   **15.** personal

SKILL DRILL 3

1. fictional   **2.** missile   **3.** commercial   **4.** several   **5.** fragile
6. double   **7.** seasonal   **8.** economical   **9.** receptacle   **10.** rehearsal
11. spectacle   **12.** personal   **13.** article   **13.** simple   **15.** survival

SKILL DRILL 4

Order of answers will vary in 1–2, 4–6, 10–12.

1. fragile   **2.** missile   **3.** double   **4.** article   **5.** receptacle
6. spectacle   **7.** commercial   **8.** survival   **9.** rehearsal   **10.** fictional
11. personal   **12.** seasonal   **13.** several   **14.** simple   **15.** economical

WORD GAME 10

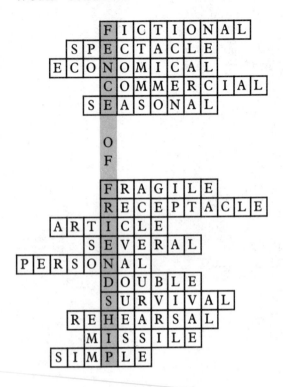

How could you describe the border between Canada and the United States? *FENCE OF FRIENDSHIP*

HOW WELL CAN YOU SPELL?

A. **1.** receptacle **2.** seasonal **3.** spectacle **4.** survival **5.** double

6. fictional **7.** missile

B. **8.** article **9.** commercial **10.** several

11. rehearsal **12.** personal

13. fragile **14.** economical **15.** simple

Optional Testing List

Lessons 6–10 (Challenge Words are italicized.)

acknowledge
adjacent
aisle
answered
antonym
application
article
artificial
assemble
avenues
axle
biscuits
bruised
buildings
circuit
civilization
commercial
condemn
confidential
crumble
crystals
cylinder
cynical
debtor
delicious
discontinue
discussion
disguise
double
doubtful
economical
encyclopedia
enlighten
exhibit
exquisite
fascinating
fictional
financial
foreigner
fragile

friendship
fruitful
graduation
gravity
guarantee
guardian
guilty
guitar
gymnasium
hydrogen
hyphen
impatient
influential
information
initial
judicial
juiciest
magician
mammal
mannequin
missile
mortgage
musician
mutual
mysterious
mythology
nuisance
numerous
official
often
oxygen
personal
physician
politician
procession
professional
pursuit
pyramids
quilted
quotient

racial
receptacle
rehearsal
rescue
residue
resemble
revenue
rhyme
rhythm
scenery
schedule
scissors
seasonal
session
several
simple
smudge
solidify
special
spectacle
stomach
subdue
suitcases
survival
syllable
symbolic
symmetrical
sympathetic
synonym
synopsis
synthetic
tissue
tongue
transition
typhoon
tyranny
unsuitable
vanished
virtues
visual

11. Run for Life

Pages 81–88

Objective

This lesson introduces *prefixes* and their role in word formation and meaning. The five used in the lesson—*con, com, dis, ac,* and *re*—are common prefixes found in hundreds of words. The teacher should encourage memorization of these prefixes and their meanings. Knowledge of prefixes and their meanings is an integral part of vocabulary development. The teacher should encourage the student to find other words with the same prefixes in order to strengthen vocabulary and spelling skills.

REVIEWING YOUR READING

1. a   2. c   3. c   4. b   5. d   6. c   7. b   8. a

FIGURING THE FACTS

Wording may vary for false answers.

1. F; 3,000   2. T   3. T   4. F; with a few friends   5. F; 36   6. T
7. F; Boston   8. T   9. T   10. T

WHAT'S YOUR OPINION?

Answers will vary.

SKILL DRILL 1

1. com/pleted	2. dis/pute	3. ac/ceptable	4. con/firm	5. re/creation
6. ac/company	7. com/mittee	8. dis/abilities	9. re/quired	10. ac/cuse
11. con/junction	12. re/commend	13. con/tribution	14. com/petition	15. dis/solve

SKILL DRILL 2

1. recreation	2. required	3. recommend	4. accompany	5. accuse
6. acceptable	7. dispute	8. disabilities	9. dissolve	10. conjunction
11. contribution	12. committee	13. competition	14. completed	15. confirm

SKILL DRILL 3

1. committee	2. competition	3. contribution	4. required	5. recommend
6. dispute	7. acceptable	8. completed	9. conjunction	10. confirm
11. recreation	12. dissolve	13. disabilities	14. accuse	15. accompany

SKILL DRILL 4

Order of answers may vary in 1–6, 7–9, 10–12, 13–15.

1. committee
2. competition
3. completed
4. confirm
5. conjunction
6. contribution
7. recommend
8. recreation
9. required
10. disabilities
11. dispute
12. dissolve
13. acceptable
14. accompany
15. accuse

WORD GAME 11

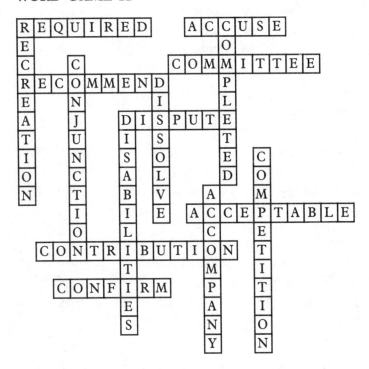

HOW WELL CAN YOU SPELL?

A.
1. acceptable
2. recreation
3. accompany
4. accuse
5. conjunction
6. dissolve
7. competition

B.
8. disabilities
9. required
10. recommend
11. dispute
12. completed
13. committee
14. confirm
15. contribution

---

12.   The Wall

Pages 89–96

Objective

This lesson introduces four new prefixes: *un*, *in*, *en*, and *sub*. As a review of the previous lesson, more words with the prefix *re* are included. The teacher should demonstrate how a knowledge of prefix meanings can help to determine the meaning of a word. At this time, it would be appropriate for the teacher to demonstrate the different shades of meaning that each prefix carries. For example, the meaning of *dis* in *disabilities* varies slightly from the meaning it implies in *dissolve*. The student should be encouraged to become familiar with the dictionary definition of each "Study List" word and attempt to use each word in his or her writing.

REVIEWING YOUR READING

1. c   **2.** a   **3.** c   **4.** d   **5.** a   **6.** a   **7.** b   **8.** c

FIGURING THE FACTS

Wording may vary for false answers.

1. F; Washington, D.C.   **2.** T   **3.** T   **4.** F; who died in the Vietnam War   **5.** T
6. T   **7.** F; college   **8.** T   **9.** T   **10.** T

WHAT'S YOUR OPINION?

Answers will vary.

SKILL DRILL 1

1. sub/terranean	**2.** en/graved	**3.** un/satisfactory	**4.** sub/mitted	**5.** re/sponsibility
6. re/spiration	**7.** in/creasingly	**8.** un/expected	**9.** en/thusiasm	**10.** en/vironment
11. re/flection	**12.** sub/stitution	**13.** in/spiring	**14.** un/necessary	**15.** in/convenient

SKILL DRILL 2

1. increasingly	**2.** environment	**3.** enthusiasm	**4.** inconvenient	**5.** substitution
6. subterranean	**7.** unexpected	**8.** unnecessary	**9.** unsatisfactory	**10.** respiration
11. engraved	**12.** reflection	**13.** submitted	**14.** inspiring	**15.** responsibility

SKILL DRILL 3

1. responsibility	**2.** submitted	**3.** unsatisfactory	**4.** engraved	**5.** inconvenient
6. inspiring	**7.** subterranean	**8.** respiration	**9.** substitution	**10.** unnecessary
11. enthusiasm	**12.** increasingly	**13.** unexpected	**14.** environment	**15.** reflection

SKILL DRILL 4

1. inconvenient	**2.** increasingly	**3.** inspiring	**4.** unexpected	**5.** unnecessary
6. unsatisfactory	**7.** engraved	**8.** enthusiasm	**9.** environment	**10.** reflection
11. respiration	**12.** responsibility	**13.** submitted	**14.** substitution	**15.** subterranean

WORD GAME 12

HOW WELL CAN YOU SPELL?

A. 1. respiration 2. substitution 3. unexpected 4. enthusiasm 5. unsatisfactory
6. reflection 7. increasingly

B. 8. submitted 9. responsibility 10. inconvenient 11. environment 12. unnecessary
13. engraved 14. inspiring 15. subterranean

---

13. Pulling Her Weight

Pages 97–104

Objective

The object of this lesson is to introduce *suffixes* and to show how a suffix can change a word from one part of speech to another. The suffixes discussed are *ous, ly,* and *ness.* The rule states that adjectives ending in *ous* can be changed to adverbs by adding the suffix *ly,* and to nouns by ending *ness.*

The teacher would be wise to use this opportunity to discuss these various parts of speech and their uses in our language. A working knowledge of adjectives, adverbs, and nouns, and their relationships to each other, can not only aid students in spelling, but also strengthen their language skills.

REVIEWING YOUR READING

1. b 2. c 3. d 4. c 5. a 6. d 7. c 8. b

FIGURING THE FACTS

Wording may vary for false answers.

1. F; more than 2. F; first 3. T 4. T 5. T 6. F; French 7. T
8. F; part-time 9. T 10. T

WHAT'S YOUR OPINION?

Answers will vary.

SKILL DRILL 1

1. ridicul(ous) 2. miscellane(ous) 3. vigor(ous)ly 4. suspici(ous)(ly) 5. courte(ous)(ly)
6. seri(ous)(ness) 7. tremend(ous)(ly) 8. nerv(ous)(ness) 9. preci(ous) 10. vari(ous)
11. studi(ous)(ness) 12. enorm(ous)(ness)13. unconsci(ous)(ly)14. previ(ous)(ly) 15. envi(ous)

SKILL DRILL 2

1. various 2. studiousness 3. seriousness 4. ridiculous 5. previously
6. precious 7. nervousness 8. envious 9. courteously 10. miscellaneous
11. vigorously 12. suspiciously 13. unconsciously 14. enormousness 15. tremendously

SKILL DRILL 3

1. courteously	2. vigorously	3. envious	4. miscellaneous	5. previously
6. seriousness	7. tremendously	8. enormousness	9. unconsciously	10. nervousness
11. precious	12. ridiculous	13. studiousness	14. various	15. suspiciously

SKILL DRILL 4

studiously	studiousness	suspicious	suspiciousness
vigorously	vigorousness	various	variousness
unconscious	unconsciously	courteously	courteousness
enormous	enormousness	envious	enviously
nervously	nervousness	precious	preciousness
previous	previously	ridiculously	ridiculousness
serious	seriousness	miscellaneously	miscellaneousness

WORD GAME 13

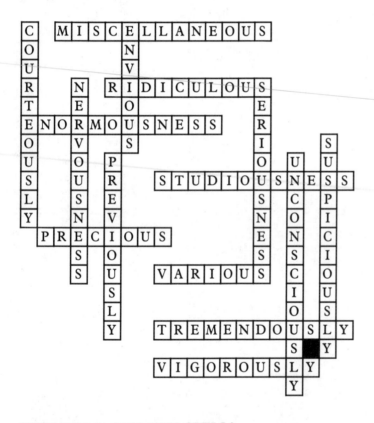

HOW WELL CAN YOU SPELL?

A.   1. unconsciously 2. enormousness 3. nervousness   4. previously   5. ridiculous
      6. suspiciously 7. seriousness

B.   8. various   9. vigorously 10. courteously 11. envious 12. miscellaneous
     13. tremendously 14. precious 15. studiousness

14. The Hero

Pages 105–112

Objective

The focus of this lesson is on the suffixes *able* and *ible*. Since these endings are often confused, we have offered a hint that if the base is a complete word, then the suffix is probably *able*. The word *remarkable* is a good example of this. However, this is not a general rule and should not be taken as such. The teacher should review the "Study List," pointing out the exceptions to this spelling hint. The exceptions in the list are *comparable*, *reliable*, and *valuable*.

REVIEWING YOUR READING

1. d   **2.** c   **3.** d   **4.** a   **5.** c   **6.** c   **7.** a   **8.** c

FIGURING THE FACTS

Wording may vary for false answers.

1. T   **2.** F; facing people   **3.** F; from books   **4.** T   **5.** T   **6.** F; early
7. T   **8.** T   **9.** F; woodworking   **10.** T

WHAT'S YOUR OPINION?

Answers will vary.

SKILL DRILL 1

1. irresist(ible)   **2.** incred(ible)   **3.** elig(ible)   **4.** compat(ible)   **5.** valu(able)
6. remark(able)   **7.** notice(able)   **8.** indel(ible)   **9.** depend(able)   **10.** compar(able)
11. consider(able)   **12.** sens(ible)   **13.** reli(able)   **14.** leg(ible)   **14.** irrespons(ible)

SKILL DRILL 2

1. valuable   **2.** reliable   **3.** dependable   **4.** indelible   **5.** comparable
6. incredible   **7.** irresistible   **8.** legible   **9.** irresponsible   **10.** considerable
11. compatible   **12.** eligible   **13.** noticeable   **14.** sensible   **15.** remarkable

SKILL DRILL 3

1. valuable   **2.** remarkable   **3.** legible   **4.** irresistible   **5.** incredible
6. eligible   **7.** compatible   **8.** sensible   **9.** noticeable   **10.** irresponsible
11. indelible   **12.** dependable   **13.** comparable   **14.** considerable   **15.** reliable

SKILL DRILL 4

Order of answers may vary in 1–2, 3–4, 5–7, 8–9, 11–12.

1. irresponsible	2. irresistible	3. incredible	4. indelible	5. compatible
6. comparable	7. considerable	8. remarkable	9. reliable	10. dependable
11. eligible	12. legible	13. valuable	14. sensible	15. noticeable

WORD GAME 14

HOW WELL CAN YOU SPELL?

A.
1. considerable	2. dependable	3. incredible	4. irresistible	5. reliable
6. remarkable	7. sensible			

B.
8. valuable	9. noticeable	10. legible	11. irresponsible	12. indelible
13. eligible	14. comparable	15. compatible		

---

15. Save Our Smiles

Pages 113–120

Objective

This lesson deals with adding the suffix *ly* or *lly* to change a word from one part of speech to another. There is a brief explanation of what a noun is and of the functions of nouns, adjectives, and adverbs. However, the teacher should provide a more in-depth review to make certain that the differences are clear to all students.

The teacher would be wise to review those words in the "Study List" that may have forms in all three categories: noun, adjective, and adverb.

REVIEWING YOUR READING

1. b   2. a   3. b   4. a   5. d   6. b   7. a   8. d

FIGURING THE FACTS

Wording may vary for false answers.

1. T   2. F; bacteria   3. T   4. T   5. T   6. F; hard   7. F; Hardened
8. F; gums   9. T   10. T

WHAT'S YOUR OPINION?

Answers will vary.

SKILL DRILL 1

1. usually	2. annually	3. typically	4. physically	5. artistically
6. generally	7. mathematically	8. logically	9. athletically	10. politically
11. musically	12. eventually	13. historically	14. basically	15. artificially

SKILL DRILL 2

1. basically	2. annually	3. usually	4. typically	5. politically
6. physically	7. athletically	8. artificially	9. artistically	10. eventually
11. generally	12. logically	13. musically	14. mathematically	15. historically

SKILL DRILL 3

Answers will vary; accept any correct noun or adjective.

1. music, musical	2. logic, logical	3. artist, artistic	4. usual	5. politics, political
6. general	7. basic	8. mathematics, mathematical	9. annual	10. history, historic, historical
11. typical	12. physical	13. eventual	14. athlete, athletic	15. artificial

SKILL DRILL 4

1. usually	2. generally	3. historically	4. logically	5. mathematically
6. musically	7. annually	8. athletically	9. basically	10. eventually
11. physically	12. politically	13. artificially	14. typically	15. artistically

WORD GAME 15

```
M A T H E M A T I C A L L Y

A R T I S T I C A L L Y
  U S U A L L Y
  B A S I C A L L Y
G E N E R A L L Y

  O
  F

A T H L E T I C A L L Y
L O G I C A L L Y
P O L I T I C A L L Y
  T Y P I C A L L Y
  H I S T O R I C A L L Y
  P H Y S I C A L L Y
  A N N U A L L Y
M U S I C A L L Y
A R T I F I C I A L L Y
    E V E N T U A L L Y
```

What is it that helps keep your teeth together? *A TUBE OF TOOTHPASTE*

HOW WELL CAN YOU SPELL?

A. **1.** athletically **2.** artistically **3.** generally **4.** logically **5.** musically

 6. physically **7.** politically **8.** annually

B. **9.** usually **10.** typically **11.** mathematically

 12. eventually **13.** artificially **14.** basically **15.** historically

Optional Testing List

Lessons 11–15 (Challenge Words are italicized.)

acceptable	basically	*consideration*
accessible	committee	contribution
accommodate	comparable	*convenience*
accompany	*comparison*	courteously
accuse	compatible	*critically*
additionally	competition	*curiously*
annually	*complaint*	*deliciousness*
anxiously	completed	dependable
apologetically	*confined*	*detectable*
artificially	confirm	*digestible*
artistically	conjunction	disabilities
athletically	considerable	dispute

138

dissolve	irresistible	respiration
distribute	irresponsible	responsibility
divisible	legible	*revolutionary*
eligible	logically	ridiculous
emotionally	*marvelously*	sensible
enchanting	mathematically	seriousness
encounter	*melodious*	*sizable*
engraved	miscellaneous	*sociable*
enlargement	musically	*strenuous*
enormousness	*nationally*	studiousness
enthusiasm	nervousness	submitted
envious	noticeable	*substantial*
environment	*patriotically*	substitution
eventually	*permissible*	subterranean
generally	physically	suspiciously
hazardous	politically	tremendously
historically	precious	typically
incidentally	previously	unconsciously
incomprehensible	*prosperous*	unexpected
inconvenient	recommend	unnecessary
increasingly	recreation	*unquestionable*
incredible	reflection	unsatisfactory
indelible	*refreshment*	*unyielding*
inflammable	reliable	usually
initially	remarkable	valuable
inspiring	*reproduce*	various
intentionally	required	*vicious*
involuntary	*resources*	vigorously

16. Champion of Children

Pages 121–128

Objective

This is the final lesson dealing with suffixes. Two sets of similar-sounding suffixes are discussed: *ance, ence,* and *ize, ise.* Since there are no rules governing these suffixes, memorization of each "Study List" word is imperative. Once again, this is an appropriate time for the student to over-emphasize the pronunciation of each list word while learning the spelling.

REVIEWING YOUR READING

1. b **2.** d **3.** a **4.** a **5.** b **6.** a **7.** b **8.** b

FIGURING THE FACTS

Wording may vary for false answers.

1. F; minister **2.** T **3.** F; South Carolina **4.** F; she has not **5.** T **6.** T
7. T **8.** F; first **9.** T **10.** T

WHAT'S YOUR OPINION?

Answers will vary.

SKILL DRILL 1

1. steril(ize) **2.** character(ize) **3.** organ(ize) **4.** comprom(ise) **5.** import(ance)
6. merchand(ise) **7.** interfer(ence) **8.** resembl(ance) **9.** circumfer(ence) **10.** modern(ize)
11. endur(ance) **12.** improv(ise) **13.** lengthw(ise) **14.** intellig(ence) **15.** influ(ence)

SKILL DRILL 2

1. circumference **2.** compromise **3.** sterilize **4.** organize **5.** modernize
6. merchandise **7.** lengthwise **8.** resemblance **9.** characterize **10.** influence
11. intelligence **12.** importance **13.** endurance **14.** improvise **15.** interference

SKILL DRILL 3

1. influence **2.** interference **3.** merchandise **4.** organize **5.** circumference
6. endurance **7.** sterilize **8.** intelligence **9.** lengthwise **10.** modernize
11. characterize **12.** compromise **13.** importance **14.** resemblance **15.** improvise

SKILL DRILL 4

Order of answers may vary in 1–3, 4–7, 8–11, 12–15.

1. endurance **2.** importance **3.** resemblance **4.** circumference **5.** intelligence
6. influence **7.** interference **8.** modernize **9.** sterilize **10.** organize
11. characterize **12.** compromise **13.** lengthwise **14.** improvise **15.** merchandise

```
                      M                               L
      E     I N T E L L I G E N C E                   E
      N           R                                   N
      D         C I R C U M F E R E N C E             G
      U         O   H                 H               T
      R E S E M B L A N C E           A   I M P R O V I S E
      A   T   P       N     M         A             S
      N   E   R       D   I M P O R T A N C E       E
      C   R   O       S       D       T
      E   I   M     I N T E R F E R E N C E
          L   I           R         R
          I   S           N         I
          Z   E     O R G A N I Z E Z
          E           N               E
      I N F L U E N C E
```

HOW WELL CAN YOU SPELL?

A. **1.** intelligence **2.** characterize **3.** resemblance **4.** modernize **5.** interference
    6. importance **7.** organize

B. **8.** lengthwise **9.** sterilize **10.** merchandise **11.** compromise **12.** endurance
    13. circumference **14.** improvise **15.** influence

---

17. Husky Victory

Pages 129–136

Objective

The focus of this lesson is on writing *numbers* and *scientific terms*. The use of the hyphen is heavily emphasized, and three rules are stated: (1) Use a hyphen when writing the compound numbers from twenty-one to ninety-nine. (2) Use a hyphen when writing the numerator and denominator in fractions. (3) Use a hyphen when writing a decimal. The teacher should point out to the student that this is not the only time hyphens are used, but they are most often used when writing numbers.

The mathematical terms are ones with which the student should already be familiar; however, the teacher should take time to explain each in order to clarify any questions the student might have.

REVIEWING YOUR READING

1. c   **2.** c   **3.** b   **4.** b   **5.** c   **6.** d   **7.** a   **8.** b

FIGURING THE FACTS

Wording may vary for false answers.

1. F; 130 miles (209 kilometers)   2. F; invisible   3. T   4. F; seventeen   5. T
6. F; twenty-two   7. T   8. T   9. F; lead dogs   10. T

WHAT'S YOUR OPINION?

Answers will vary.

WORD GAME 17

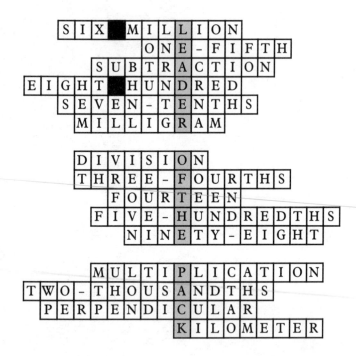

What do you call the smartest animal on a dog sled team? the *LEADER OF THE PACK*

HOW WELL CAN YOU SPELL?

A.   1. division   2. eight hundred   3. five-hundredths   4. fourteen   5. milligram
     6. seven-tenths   7. two-thousandths

B.   8. Multiplication   9. ninety-eight   10. perpendicular   11. million   12. kilometer
     13. subtraction   14. Three-fourths   15. one-fifth

SKILL DRILL 1

Answers should appear exactly as written in the exercise.

SKILL DRILL 2

A. 1. one-fifth 2. seven-tenths 3. eight hundred 4. two-thousandths 5. three-fourths
6. five-hundredths 7. fourteen 8. ninety-eight 9. six million

B. 10. division 11. multiplication 12. subtraction 13. kilometer 14. milligram
15. perpendicular

SKILL DRILL 3

1. fourteen 2. milligram 3. ninety-eight 4. perpendicular 5. six million
6. eight hundred 7. subtraction 8. kilometer 9. multiplication 10. one-fifth
11. seven-tenths 12. division 13. five-hundreths 14. three-fourths 15. two-thousandths

SKILL DRILL 4

Order of answers may vary in 1–3, 4–8, 9–11, 12–13.

1. eight hundred 2. six million 3. fourteen 4. one-fifth 5. three-fourths
6. seven-tenths 7. two-thousandths 8. five-hundredths 9. subtraction 10. division
11. multiplication 12. kilometer 13. milligram 14. perpendicular 15. ninety-eight

---

18. Big Bird

Pages 137–144

Objective

The focus of this lesson is on *dictionary entries*. The emphasis is on guide words; however, definitions, pronunciation, and other dictionary features are discussed as well. The teacher should encourage students to become familiar with their dictionaries and to look up any words that have unfamiliar spellings. Very often, students are reluctant to look up words because of the time it takes to find a particular word. Therefore, it is most important to stress the use of guide words when consulting the dictionary. As part of the lesson, the teacher should assign the task of looking up the "Study List" words and citing the guide words for each.

REVIEWING YOUR READING

1. c 2. a 3. d 4. d 5. a 6. b 7. a 8. c

FIGURING THE FACTS

1. T 2. T 3. F; ultra-light 4. F; 36 feet 5. F; flight 6. F; Texas
7. F; largest 8. T 9. F; smaller 10. T

WHAT'S YOUR OPINION?

Answers will vary.

SKILL DRILL 1

1. congratulations	2. indefinitely	3. performance	4. surrounded	5. absence
6. analyze	7. equivalent	8. emergency	9. magnificent	10. situation
11. undoubtedly	12. accurate	13. coincidence	14. essential	15. guidance

SKILL DRILL 1

Answers should appear exactly as written in the exercise; circled letters will vary.

SKILL DRILL 2

1. performance	2. magnificent	3. undoubtedly	4. absence	5. accurate
6. essential	7. equivalent	8. emergency	9. congratulations	10. surrounded
11. indefinitely	12. situation	13. coincidence	14. guidance	15. analyze

SKILL DRILL 3

1. absence	2. emergency	3. coincidence	4. accurate	5. congratulations
6. analyze	7. equivalent	8. essential	9. guidance	10. indefinitely
11. surrounded	12. magnificent	13. situation	14. performance	15. undoubtedly

SKILL DRILL 4

1. situation	2. surrounded	3. undoubtedly	4. analyze	5. coincidence
6. emergency	7. equivalent	8. essential	9. congratulations	10. absence
11. accurate	12. guidance	13. indefinitely	14. magnificent	15. performance

WORD GAME 18

HOW WELL CAN YOU SPELL?

A.
1. undoubtedly
2. situation
3. magnificent
4. guidance
5. equivalent
6. congratulations
7. analyze

B.
8. absence
9. surrounded
10. performance
11. indefinitely
12. essential
13. emergency
14. coincidence
15. accurate

---

19. Listening to Eudora

Pages 145–152

Objective

The words listed in this lesson are among the most commonly misspelled words in the English language. Therefore, we refer to these words as "spelling demons." The use of mnemonics should be particularly encouraged here. The emphasis should be on the student's careful examination of each "Study List" word, while making mental notes on what is odd or unusual about the spelling of each. Once again, the best way for the students to learn the word is to make it an active part of their written vocabulary by using it in their writing.

REVIEWING YOUR READING

1. b
2. a
3. c
4. b
5. c
6. c
7. b
8. c

FIGURING THE FACTS

Wording may vary for false answers.
1. T
2. F; 75th
3. F; Mississippi
4. F; her father
5. T
6. T
7. T
8. T
9. F; school paper
10. T

WHAT'S YOUR OPINION?

Answers will vary.

SKILL DRILL 1

Answers should appear exactly as written in the exercise; circled letters will vary.

SKILL DRILL 2

1. permanent
2. autobiography
3. admiration
4. appropriate
5. association
6. imaginary
7. immediately
8. independent
9. interpretation
10. occasion
11. possession
12. preferred
13. literary
14. embarrassed
15. continuous

SKILL DRILL 3

1. immediately
2. embarrassed
3. autobiography
4. appropriate
5. preferred
6. permanent
7. literary
8. imaginary
9. continuous
10. association
11. admiration
12. possession
13. occasion
14. interpretation
15. independent

SKILL DRILL 4

Order of answers may vary in 1–5, 6–7, 8–10, 11–13.

1. association
2. admiration
3. possession
4. interpretation
5. occasion
6. independent
7. permanent
8. immediately
9. imaginary
10. embarrassed
11. autobiography
12. continuous
13. preferred
14. appropriate
15. literary

WORD GAME 19

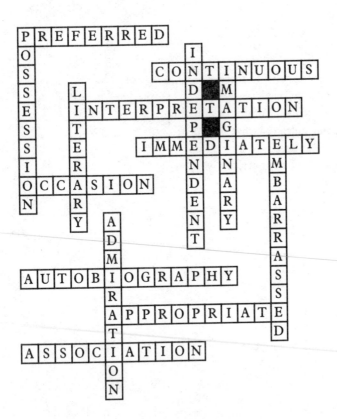

HOW WELL CAN YOU SPELL?

A.
1. continuous
2. association
3. independent
4. interpretation
5. possession
6. permanent
7. appropriate

B.
8. preferred
9. occasion
10. literary
11. immediately
12. imaginary
13. embarrassed
14. autobiography
15. admiration

20. Tree People

Pages 153–160

Objective

As in the previous lesson, the focus here is on frequently misspelled words, or "spelling demons." The lesson takes the student through a process of word analysis and written drills, but this may not be enough to facilitate proper spelling. The student should be encouraged to find out what it is that makes each word difficult to spell, to memorize the correct spelling, and to use each word in his or her writing.

REVIEWING YOUR READING

1. b   2. a   3. c   4. a   5. a   6. c   7. d   8. a

FIGURING THE FACTS

Wording may vary for false answers.

1. T   2. F; young   3. T   4. T   5. T   6. T   7. F; one million   8. T
9. F; prevent   10. T

WHAT'S YOUR OPINION?

Answers will vary.

SKILL DRILL 1

Answers should appear exactly as written in the exercise; circled letters will vary.

SKILL DRILL 2

1. omitted	2. sophomore	3. maintenance	4. government	5. questionnaire
6. campaign	7. procedure	8. straighten	9. volunteer	10. calendar
11. erosion	12. pollution	13. interesting	14. mischief	15. pronunciation

SKILL DRILL 3

1. sophomore	2. pollution	3. maintenance	4. government	5. calendar
6. questionnaire	7. procedure	8. volunteer	9. omitted	10. mischief
11. interesting	12. pronunciation	13. straighten	14. erosion	15. campaign

SKILL DRILL 4

Order of answers may vary in 1–3, 4–6.

1. erosion	2. pollution	3. pronunciation	4. procedure	5. questionnaire
6. sophomore	7. volunteer	8. calendar	9. mischief	10. interesting
11. maintenance	12. campaign	13. straighten	14. omitted	15. government

WORD GAME 20

HOW WELL CAN YOU SPELL?

A.   1. pronunciation   2. campaign   3. government   4. maintenance   5. pollution
   6. procedure   7. sophomore

B.   8. volunteer   9. straighten   10. questionnaire   11. omitted   12. mischief
   13. interesting   14. erosion   15. calendar

Optional Testing List

Lessons 16–20 (Challenge Words are italicized.)

absence	*centimeter*	*criticism*
absolutely	characterize	*decimeter*
accidentally	circumference	*decision*
accurate	*circumstances*	division
acquaintance	*civilize*	eight hundred
admiration	*clockwise*	embarrassed
analyze	coincidence	emergency
appropriate	*colonize*	endurance
association	*column*	equivalent
autobiography	compromise	erosion
calendar	*conference*	essential
campaign	congratulations	*fertilize*
catalog	continuous	five-hundredths

fourteen
fulfill
furniture
government
guidance
imaginary
immediately
importance
improvise
indefinitely
independent
influence
ingenious
inheritance
innocence
instrument
intelligence
interesting
interference
interpretation
kilometer
laboratory
lengthwise
lightning
literary
loneliness
magnificent

maintenance
merchandise
microscope
milligram
milliliter
miniature
mischief
modernize
multiplication
ninety-eight
occasion
omission
ommitted
one-fifth
organize
parallel
particularly
patience
performance
permanent
perpendicular
persuade
pollution
polygon
possession
practically
practice

preferred
privilege
procedure
pronunciation
quadrilateral
questionnaire
remembrance
resemblance
resistance
sacrifice
seven-tenths
situation
six-million
sophomores
sterilize
straighten
subtraction
surrounded
televise
tendency
thermometer
three-fourths
trapezoid
two-thousandths
undoubtedly
unmanageable
volunteer

Supplementary Words

A PARTIAL LIST OF EASY SPELLING WORDS

abandon	captain	February	needle	quiet	target
ache	catalog (or	flour	nevertheless		thankful
address	catalogue)	function	nickel	rapid	thorough
agreeable	clothes			region	tremble
all right	comfortable	government	occur	retreat	truly
approach	committee	grease	o'clock		
	cough			sandwich	untie
balance	curtain	height	pajamas	similar	
bicycle			permit	sincerely	value
breathe	dairy	kettle	picnic	skiing	
brilliant	depot		pitcher	suppose	wrong
bulletin	diary	laughter	possible		
	doorknob	liniment	presence		yield
			principal		
	excellent	mystery			zinc

149

A PARTIAL LIST OF MORE DIFFICULT SPELLING WORDS

absence	calendar	emergency	magazine	quarter	temperature
absolutely	campaign		marriage		tendency
acceptable	celebration	forth	measles	receipt	threshold
aisle	cemetery		mosquito	recipe	tongue
alcohol	chimney	gnat		rhythm	
anniversary	column		niece		vacuum
approximately	conquer	hiccup		satellite	vegetable
athlete	cooperate	hymn	occurred	separate	villain
awkward	crystal		opposite	shield	
	cupful	judgment		shiny	wrist
banquet			persuade	shrew	
barbecue	debris	license (or	physics	signature	zither
blossom	debt	licence	picnicking		
buoy	deceive		pier		
	definite		professor		

A PARTIAL LIST OF CHALLENGE SPELLING WORDS

accompanied	colonel	gauge	neighbor	receive	tantalize
acquire	concede	gnu	nucleus	reign	tragedy
adjustment	condemn			repetition	turbulence
adolescent	Connecticut	hundredth	oblige		
amateur	courteous			scandal	unanimous
ammunition	crepe	icicle	pamphlet	scribbling	unique
ancient	criticism	irrelevant	parallel	seize	
Antarctic			peninsula	solemn	vengeance
authentic	dessert	knowledge	phenomenon	spacious	
			plateau	spaghetti	wooly (or woolly)
biscuit	embarrass	leisure	pneumonia	surveyor	wrought
bologna	enthusiastic		privilege	syllable	
bough		minstrel	proceed		
	ferocious	mischievous	psalm		
	fulfillment		psychology		

A PARTIAL LIST OF EXPERT SPELLING WORDS

abundance	bazaar	dirigible	gorgeous	pageant	tarpaulin
accommodation	beige	discipline		paraffin	transcendental
accordance	beneficiary	dissimilar	harangue	pasteurize	translucent
acquaint	bouillon	drought	heinous	phlegm	travois
adequate	boulevard		hygiene	precipitation	
advantageous		emabarrassment			vicious
affidavit	caffeine	exaggerate	irresistible	queue	weird
aluminum	chamois	expenditure			
analysis	chrysanthemum		maneuver	requisition	xylophone
annihilate	competent	facetious	mayonnaise	rheumatism	
apostrophe	conscience	facsimile	Milwaukee		Zaire
argument	crochet	fascist		schedule	
autumn		foreign	nuisance	soliloguy	
		furlough		surveillance	
			ophthalmologist		